HIDDEN HISTORY
of
WESTERN KENTUCKY

Berry Craig

Published by The History Press
Charleston, SC 29403
www.historypress.net

Copyright © 2011 by Berry Craig
All rights reserved

Images are courtesy of the author unless otherwise noted.

First published 2011

Manufactured in the United States

ISBN 978.1.60949.397.4

Library of Congress Cataloging-in-Publication Data

Craig, Berry.
Hidden history of western Kentucky / Berry Craig.
p. cm.
ISBN 978-1-60949-397-4
1. Kentucky--History--Anecdotes. 2. Kentucky--Social life and customs--Anecdotes. 3. Kentucky--Biography--Anecdotes. I. Title.
F451.6.C727 2011
976.9'7--dc23
2011039788

Notice: The information in this book is true and complete to the best of our knowledge. It is offered without guarantee on the part of the author or The History Press. The author and The History Press disclaim all liability in connection with the use of this book.

All rights reserved. No part of this book may be reproduced or transmitted in any form whatsoever without prior written permission from the publisher except in the case of brief quotations embodied in critical articles and reviews.

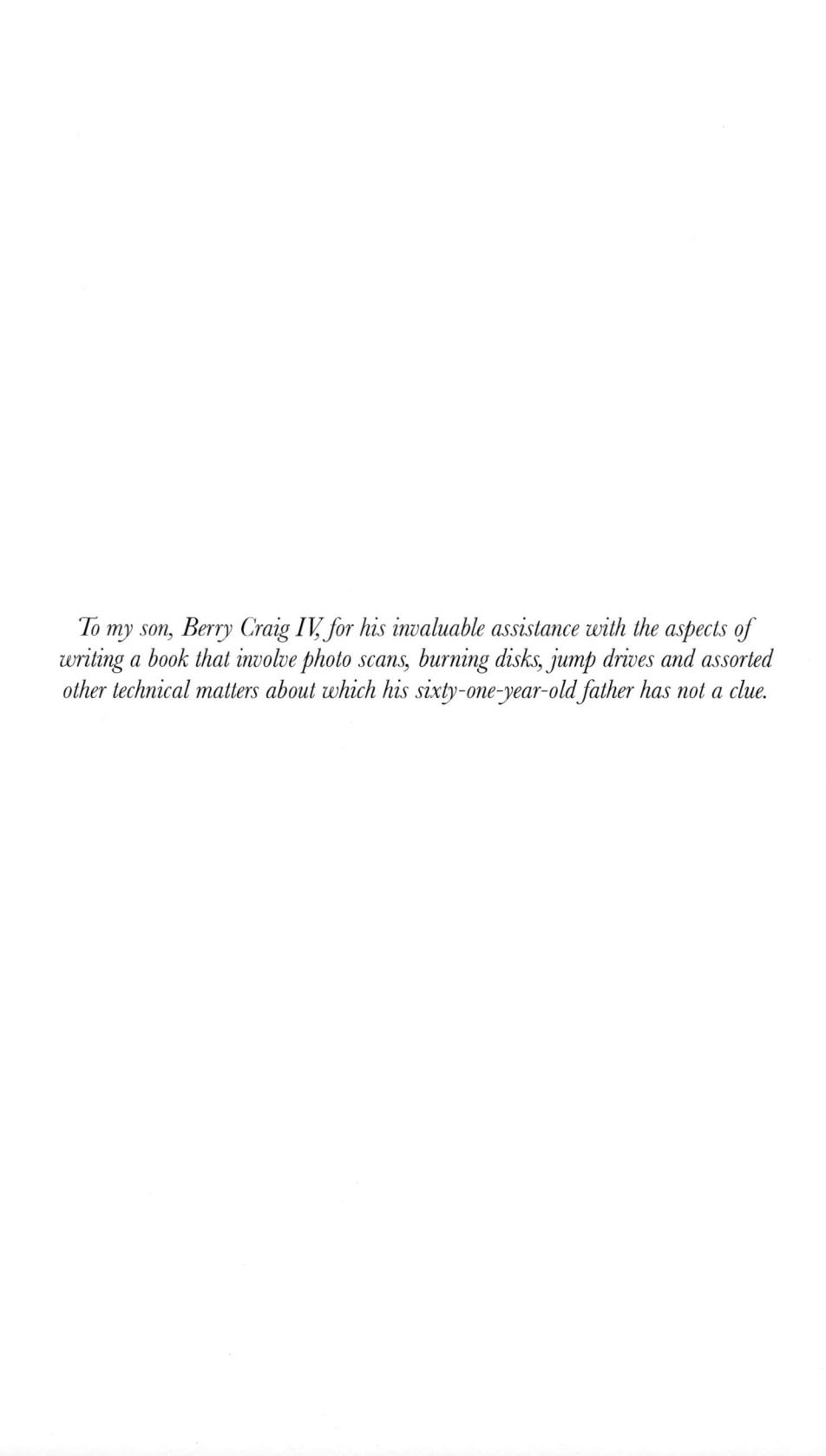

To my son, Berry Craig IV, for his invaluable assistance with the aspects of writing a book that involve photo scans, burning disks, jump drives and assorted other technical matters about which his sixty-one-year-old father has not a clue.

Contents

1. The Famous and Not So Famous　　7
2. Outright Villains and Other Shady Characters　　55
3. Tragedies　　73
4. Gone but Not Forgotten　　93
5. Towns and Their Roots　　105
6. Really Hidden History　　115

About the Author　　143

I
The Famous and Not So Famous

"To the Shores of Tripoli"

There is a western Kentucky connection to the "Marines' Hymn." The part that goes "To the shores of Tripoli" commemorates U.S. Marines who whipped the Barbary Pirates of North Africa in 1805. Their leader was Virginia-born Lieutenant Presley O'Bannon, who ended up in Russellville, where his old two-story brick home is still a dwelling. A front-yard historical marker says that he was "the first American to raise our flag on foreign soil."

O'Bannon also served in the Kentucky House of Representatives and Senate before he died in 1850 at age seventy-four. He is buried in the Frankfort Cemetery, where another marker says he was the "first American to raise the U.S. flag on foreign soil."

The pirates menaced merchant ships in the Mediterranean. The buccaneers not only captured cargo vessels, but they also enslaved sailors or held them for ransom. Reputedly, the brigands obeyed only "the laws of prey as practiced by wild animals."

In 1795, Congress paid the North African Barbary states $1 million to free U.S. hostages. When the Barbary rulers demanded more money early in President Thomas Jefferson's administration, he ordered American warships to blockade the state of Tripoli, now Libya, a major pirate haven. Next came one of the most colorful episodes in U.S. military history.

HIDDEN HISTORY OF WESTERN KENTUCKY

Above: Presley O'Bannon's brick home in Russellville.

Left: O'Bannon's grave in the Frankfort Cemetery.

The Famous and Not So Famous

In 1805, William Eaton, U.S. consul in Tunis, raised a multinational army to seize the Tripolitan seaport of Derna. He chose O'Bannon, twenty-nine, to command the force, which accomplished its mission.

In his book *The Wars of America*, historian Robert Leckie wrote that Eaton and O'Bannon marched across the sweltering Sahara from Egypt to Derna at the head of "6 or 7 other marines, a naval midshipman, 40 Greeks, 100 of the flotsam of Europe and Asia coughed up on the shores of the Levant, a squadron of mounted Arabs...and a fleet of camels."

The ragtag army trekked five hundred miles, braving "burning sands and brazen sun," and reached Derna in fifty-one days. Bone-weary and sun-baked, O'Bannon called on the fortress town's top official, the Bey of Derna, to surrender, Leckie wrote.

"My head or yours," the Bey replied. Backed up by a trio of U.S. warships, O'Bannon and his men stormed the city, forcing the Bey to give up.

With the fall of Derna, Tripoli agreed to peace terms. But other Barbary Pirates continued to plunder American ships and exact tribute until 1816.

"MY FIRST IMPULSE WAS TO THROW MYSELF ON THE GROUND"

"So you're the little woman who wrote the book that started this great war," Abraham Lincoln supposedly said to Harriet Beecher Stowe when they met.

Stowe wrote *Uncle Tom's Cabin; or, Life Among the Lowly*, one of the most famous novels in American history. If Uncle Tom, the main character, seemed especially real, he evidently was.

"Uncle Tom Lived Here," says a state historical marker on U.S. Highway 60—the "Josiah Henson Trail"—near Maceo in Daviess County. "Site of Riley family homeplace, owners of Josiah Henson, one of the characters on which Harriet Beecher Stowe based her 1852 novel *Uncle Tom's Cabin*."

Henson led his family to freedom in Canada in 1830. "Henson served as overseer of Amos Riley's farms, 1825–29," the marker explains. "On learning owner planned to sell him 'down the river,' he escaped to Canada, living there rest of life."

The metal plaque also says that Stowe invited Henson to see her in Andover, Massachusetts, in 1849. "When he met Harriet Beecher Stowe, he supplied her with details of his own experience of forty-one years as a slave," said Barbara Carter, Henson's great-great-granddaughter. She has retired as manager of the Uncle Tom's Cabin Historic Site near Dresden, Ontario, where her

Reverend Josiah Henson. *Courtesy of the Library of Congress.*

ancestor settled his family and started the Dawn community for other runaway slaves.

"Harriet Beecher Stowe used Josiah Henson's memoirs, published in 1849, as reference material for her novel," said Steven Cook, who followed Carter as site manager. "Henson's dramatic experiences and his connection with Stowe's book made him one of the most famous Canadians of his day."

Henson's 1849 autobiography, *The Life of Josiah Henson, Formerly a Slave, Now an Inhabitant of Canada, as Narrated by Himself*, was republished in 1858 as *Truth Stranger than Fiction, Father Henson's Story of His Life*. A third version, *Uncle Tom's Story of His Life: An Autobiography of the Rev. Josiah Henson*, appeared in 1876. The first memoir made Henson well known among American abolitionists, including Stowe, whose best-selling book converted thousands of Northerners to the antislavery cause.

Also a Methodist minister and Canadian militia captain, Henson joined the secret Underground Railroad. He and other "conductors," white and African American, assisted many slaves in their flights to freedom.

Henson, who was born in Maryland about 1796, risked his own freedom by slipping back into the American slave states and helping 118 other slaves escape from "the cruel and merciless grasp of the slaveholder," he wrote.

In *From Slavery to Freedom: A History of African Americans*, John Hope Franklin wrote that Henson once returned to Kentucky via "a circuitous route through New York, Pennsylvania, and Ohio to avoid suspicion. He took thirty refugees out of Kentucky and led them to Toledo within a period of two weeks."

To help finance the Dawn settlement, Henson traveled widely, lecturing against slavery in the U.S. free states and Canada. He even took his cause to England.

The Famous and Not So Famous

Josiah Henson Trail in Daviess County.

His speeches and his books recounted the astonishing story of how he and his family escaped bondage on a moonless night in mid-September 1830. They journeyed five hundred miles to Canada, almost all of the way on foot. Often, they traveled at night to avoid capture.

Henson carefully planned his break for freedom with his wife and their four children. He explained in his 1849 autobiography:

> *Some time previously I had got my wife to make me a large knapsack, big enough to hold the two smallest children; and I had arranged it that she should lead the second boy, while the oldest was stout enough to go by himself, and to help me carry the necessary food. I used to pack the little ones on my back, of an evening, after I had got through my day's work, and trot round the cabin with them, and go some little distance from it, in order to accustom both them and myself to the task before us.*

On the appointed night, the Hensons walked to the nearby Ohio River. Another slave waited in a skiff to ferry them to the free state of Indiana. Henson recalled:

> *It was an agitating and solemn moment. The good fellow who was rowing us over, said this affair might end in his death; "but," said he, "you will*

not be brought back alive, will you?" "Not if I can help it," I answered. "And if you are overpowered and return," he asked, "will you conceal my part of the business?" "That I will, so help me God," I replied. "Then I am easy," he answered, "and wish you success."

The family reached the Indiana shore, where Henson said he "began to feel that I was my own master." But they were not out of danger.

Slave catchers patrolled the river on the Indiana side. Many whites who lived in the area were proslavery and happy to help the slave catchers.

"We were to travel by night, and rest by day, in the woods and bushes," Henson remembered. "We were thrown absolutely upon our own poor and small resources, and were to rely on our own strength alone."

It took the Hensons two weeks to reach Cincinnati, an antislavery center. "There we were kindly received and entertained for several days, my wife and little ones were refreshed, and then we were carried on our way thirty miles in a wagon," he wrote.

As they headed north through southern Ohio, the family "followed the same course as before, of travelling by night, and resting by day, till we arrived at the Scioto [River], where we had been told we should strike the military road of General Hull, in the last war with Great Britain, and might then safely travel by day," he wrote. "We found the road, accordingly, by the large sycamore and elm which marked its beginning, and entered upon it with fresh spirits early in the day."

Henson said they did not know that the old military road was little more than a dirt track through a largely unpopulated wilderness. "I had neglected to provide any food, thinking we should soon come to some habitation, where we could be supplied."

Henson said they walked all one day without seeing a soul, then lay down to sleep, hungry and weary:

> *I thought I heard the howling of wolves, and the terror inspired by this, and the exertions I used to keep them off, by making as much noise as I could, took away all power of sleeping, till day-light, and rendered a little delay inevitable. In the morning we were as hungry as ever, but had nothing to relieve our appetites but a little piece of dried beef. I divided some of this all round, and then started for a second day's trip in the wilderness. It was a hard trial, and this day is a memorable one in my life.*

The Famous and Not So Famous

The dirt road was rough from disuse and neglect. Many trees had fallen across the right of way. "The underbrush was somewhat cleared away, and that was about all to mark the track."

Suddenly, Henson was seized with dread:

> *As we went wearily on, I was a little ahead of my wife and the boys, when I heard them call to me, and, turning round, saw that my wife had fallen over a log, and was prostrate on the ground. "Mother's dying," cried Tom; and when I reached her, it seemed really so. She had fainted. I did not know but it might be fatal, and was half distracted with the fear and the uncertainty. In a few minutes, however, she recovered sufficiently to take a few mouthfuls of the beef, and this, with a little rest, revived her so much that she bravely set out once more.*

The Hensons had trudged only a short distance when they spied a group of men heading toward them on the road:

> *We were instantly on the alert, as we could hardly expect them to be friends. The advance of a few paces showed me they were Indians, with packs on their shoulders; and they were so near that if they were hostile, it would be useless to try to escape. So I walked along boldly, till we came close upon them.*

The Hensons scared the Native Americans:

> *They were bent down with their burdens, and had not raised their eyes till now; and when they did so, and saw me coming towards them, they looked at me in a frightened sort of way for a moment, and then, setting up a peculiar howl, turned round, and ran as fast as they could. There were three or four of them, and what they were afraid of I could not imagine, unless they supposed I was the devil, whom they had perhaps heard of as black.*

Henson said he thought his wife and children would have reassured them:

> *However, there was no doubt they were well frightened, and we heard their wild and prolonged howl, as they ran, for a mile or more. My wife was alarmed too, and thought they were merely running back to collect more of a party, and then to come and murder us, and she wanted to turn back. I told her they were numerous enough to do that, if they wanted to, without*

help; and that as for turning back, I had had quite too much of the road behind us, and that it would be a ridiculous thing that both parties should run away. If they were disposed to run, I would follow.

The Hensons pressed on, and the forest grew silent. But they spotted the Indians peering at them from behind the trees and ducking out of sight if they thought they were visible to the family.

The Hensons reached a Native American village "and saw a fine looking, stately Indian, with his arms folded, waiting for us to approach." Henson explained:

He was apparently the chief, and, saluting us civilly, he soon discovered that we were human beings, and spoke to his young men, who were scattered about, and made them come in, and give up their foolish fears. And now curiosity seemed to prevail.

He recalled that each of the Native Americans wanted to touch his children, "who were shy as partridges, with their long life in the woods; and as they shrunk away, and uttered a little cry of alarm, the Indian would jump back too, as if he thought they would bite him."

In the end, friendship overcame fear:

A little while sufficed to make them understand what we were, and whither we were going, and what we needed; and as little, to set them about supplying our wants, feeding us bountifully, and giving us a comfortable wigwam for our night's rest. The next day we resumed our march, and found, from the Indians, that we were only about twenty-five miles from the lake. They sent some of their young men to point out the place where we were to turn off, and parted from us with as much kindness as possible.

Finally, the Hensons neared Lake Erie, where, he wrote, "we came to a spot overflowed by a stream, across which the road passed." The water was 100 to 150 yards across and as deep as four feet.

Henson forded first, aided by "a sounding pole." Afterward, he returned for the rest of his family, carrying the children on his back, from which "the skin was worn…to an extent almost equal to the size of my knapsack."

After another night spent in the woods, the family emerged onto a treeless plain south and west of Sandusky, on Lake Erie. Henson recalled:

The Famous and Not So Famous

We saw the houses of the village, and kept away from them for the present, till I should have an opportunity to reconnoitre a little. When about a mile from the lake, I hid my companions in the bushes, and pushed forward. Before I had gone far, I observed on the left, on the opposite side from the town, something which looked like a house, between which and a vessel, a number of men were passing and repassing with activity.

As Henson approached the men, one of them called out and asked him if he wanted a job. "I told him yes; and it was scarcely a minute before I had hold of a bag of corn, which, like the rest, I emptied into the hold of the vessel lying at anchor a few rods off," Henson said.

One of the workers was African American. Henson asked him where the ship was headed, what was the best route to Canada and who was the captain. Henson said he also sought "other particulars interesting to me."

He confided to the man where he had come from and where he wanted to go. The African American told the captain, who called Henson aside. "By his frank look and manner [he] soon induced me to acknowledge my condition and purpose," Henson wrote. "I found I had not mistaken him. He sympathized with me, at once, most heartily."

"The captain had agreed to send a boat for me, after sundown, rather than take me on board at the landing; as there were Kentucky spies, he said, on the watch for slaves, at Sandusky, who might get a glimpse of me, if I brought my party out of the bush by daylight," Henson explained.

He watched the ship set sail, confessing he "began to fear she would go without me." But as promised, the captain sent a boat crewed by "my black friend and two sailors."

The quartet set out to get Henson's wife and children. Again, what must have been near-panic gripped him. They were gone from where he had left them:

For a moment my fears were overpowering; but I soon discerned them, in the fading twilight, at no great distance. My wife had been alarmed by my long absence, and thought I must have been discovered by some of our watchful enemies, and had given up all for lost. Her fears were not removed by seeing me returning with three other men; and she tried to hide herself. It was not without difficulty that I satisfied her all was right, for her agitation was so great that she could not, at once, understand what I said.

Henson said the kindness of the crewmen reassured his wife. Soon the family was in the boat with the sailors heading for the ship. "A short row brought us to the vessel, and, to my astonishment, we were welcomed on board, with three hearty cheers; for the crew were as much pleased as the captain, with the help they were giving us to escape."

The ship arrived in Buffalo the next evening. But it was too late for the Hensons to cross over to Canada that night. Still, the family's journey to freedom was almost over:

> *The next morning we dropped down to Black Rock, and the friendly captain, whose name I have gratefully remembered as Captain Burnham, put us on board the ferry-boat to Waterloo, paid the passage money, and gave me a dollar at parting. He was a Scotchman, and had done enough to win my enduring gratitude, to prove himself a kind and generous man, and to give me a pleasant association with his dialect and his country.*

The family reached Canada on the morning of October 18. Henson was overjoyed:

> *My first impulse was to throw myself on the ground, and giving way to the riotous exultation of my feelings, to execute sundry antics which excited the astonishment of those who were looking on. A gentleman of the neighborhood, Colonel Warren, who happened to be present, thought I was in a fit, and as he inquired what was the matter with the poor fellow, I jumped up and told him I was free. "O," said he, with a hearty laugh, "is that it? I never knew freedom to make a man roll in the sand before."*

Henson said he hugged and kissed his wife and offspring, "which made them laugh as well as myself." But he added, "There was not much time to be lost, though, in frolic, even at this extraordinary moment. I was a stranger, in a strange land, and had to look about me at once, for refuge and resource."

He found both. At first, the family settled near Fort Erie, where he worked for a local farmer. Next, the Hensons moved to Colchester, where they lived for seven years.

But Henson wanted to own land. So in 1841, he bought a small tract near Dresden, about seventy-five miles from Detroit, and organized the Dawn settlement.

"Under his leadership, the British-American Institute, one of Canada's first industrial schools, was founded at the settlement," Carter said.

Henson died in 1883 and was buried in the family cemetery on the original Dawn property. "His grave is visited annually by thousands," Carter said.

On the centennial of his death, Henson became the first person of African descent to be featured on a Canadian postage stamp. In 1999, the Canadian government put up a metal plaque in the cemetery designating Henson as a Canadian of national historical significance.

The inscription, in English and French, Canada's two official languages, says, "His fame grew after Harriet Beecher Stowe stated that his memoirs published in 1849 had provided 'conceptions and incidents' for her extraordinarily popular novel *Uncle Tom's Cabin*. Henson's celebrity raised international awareness of Canada's reputation as a haven for refugees from slavery."

The Uncle Tom's Cabin Historic Site is an open-air museum and African American history center owned by the Ontario Heritage Trust. Besides the family cemetery, the park encompasses the Henson cabin; an interpretive center; a sawmill; a smokehouse; an 1850s vintage church, including a pulpit from which Henson preached; and the Harris House, one of the last stops on the Underground Railroad. The British-American Institute and the Dawn settlement burial ground are across the road from the park.

"Crazy" Kelly

A mysterious Englishman arrives at Suwanee Iron Furnace eager to learn about "crazy" William Kelly's secret method for making steel. The unsuspecting Kelly hires the man and a companion who came with him. After stealing Kelly's idea, the man, along with his accomplice, sneaks home to England, where fame, fortune and knighthood await him as the "father of steel."

The stranger was Sir Henry Bessemer, or so the story was told in Suwanee, a tiny Lyon County community that was a center of western Kentucky's once thriving iron industry. "Kelly said Bessemer was one of the Englishmen," said Corrine Whitehead, a local historian. "Bessemer's process was almost identical to Kelly's."

For years, history books cited Bessemer as the inventor of the process of turning iron into steel. Today, many historians credit Kelly, too.

The *Kentucky Encyclopedia* says that Kelly came up with "the 'air boiling' process of steel production." But the book is mum about Bessemer's purported purloining of Kelly's process. Bessemer denied that he swiped Kelly's idea.

Whitehead said she researched old books, records and documents about Kelly and is "absolutely convinced the story is true." She wrote about Kelly in the *Journal of the Jackson Purchase Historical Society*.

Kelly marker and kettle in Kuttawa.

Kelly was born to Irish immigrant parents "of moderate means" near Pittsburgh in 1811, according to *Profiles of the Past*, a book by Odell Walker, a Lyon County historian.

"Pittsburgh was already the iron capital of our young nation," he wrote. "It is believed, but not documented, that…William must have in some capacity learned the iron making trade in young life. It is unlikely that he was a total novice when he entered the iron industry in the 1840s in Caldwell County, now Lyon County."

On a trip to Nashville in 1845, Kelly met Mildred Gracie, the daughter of a wealthy citizen of Eddyville, the Lyon County seat. William and Mildred fell in love, married and settled in her hometown.

Kelly's brother, John, came from Pittsburgh and, with financial help from Mildred's father, went into the iron business. John and William bought the stone-walled Eddyville furnace, the first furnace built in the county. Walker wrote:

> *William Kelly was an iron genius, a thinker, an experimenter, and a tinkerer with new ideas. He was not content to be satisfied with the way iron had*

been made for four thousand years. He had a dream that iron could be made better and cheaper.

Supposedly, Kelly discovered his revolutionary steel-making process by accident. Walker explained:

> There is...an unconfirmed story that I have heard from childhood that on one occasion during a blast the furnace was overfilled and some of the molten iron ran out on the ground through a crack at the top of the furnace and hardened.
>
> Kelly took his sledge hammer to break the iron and found that it did not break easily and had some flexibility like steel. It is said... that Kelly concluded from this accident that to force a blast of cold air into molten metal, the oxygen in the air combined with the carbon in molten iron generated great heat that expelled the carbon. This was the basic principle that Kelly experimented with and developed the steel converter. This break-through made the production of steel faster and cheaper, therefore the country and the world moved from the iron age to the steel age.

After he opened the brick, thirty-five-foot-tall Suwanee furnace in 1847, Kelly devised what he called "air boiling"—the blowing of air through molten iron to burn out impurities and create steel. "People thought he was crazy," Whitehead said.

Kelly's rich father-in-law thought the iron maker had lost his mind. So did other iron makers. Kelly was dubbed "Crazy" Kelly.

"The family physician, Dr. George M. Huggans, was called upon to examine William Kelly and make a judgment on his mental fitness," Walker wrote. "Here William Kelly gained his first support, not only did Dr. Huggans declare William Kelly's mental faculties normal, but further stated that the process he espoused had merit."

Kelly continued his experiments in steelmaking, Walker wrote. In 1851, Kelly produced his first steel.

Word spread, eventually to England and supposedly to an iron maker named Bessemer, who allegedly schemed to steal Kelly's idea.

Bessemer and his abettor traveled to America by ship and then made their way to Kelly, under the guise of merely seeking jobs. After gaining Kelly's confidence and learning the "air boiling" technique, Bessemer and his friend left, according to the story.

"They didn't bother to collect wages owed them, and that made Kelly suspicious," Whitehead said. "Kelly sent bloodhounds after them." The trail turned cold at the Cumberland River, a short way from the furnace.

Kelly said he traced the strangers to Pittsburgh, New York, and, finally, to England. "A Detroit ironmaster offered to lend Kelly money so he could go to England and expose Bessemer," Whitehead said. "He didn't go because it was absolutely futile."

Walker included the tale in his book. But he suspects the men were spies sent by Bessemer.

In 1855, Bessemer got a British patent for what became known as the "Bessemer Process." A U.S. patent followed in 1856.

Kelly challenged Bessemer. "In 1857, the U.S. Patent Office gave Kelly prior patent rights," Whitehead said. "They agreed he discovered the process, not Bessemer."

Even so, Kelly's iron business eventually went broke. The Suwanee furnace was torn down; its bricks were used for bridge supports and building foundations, according to Whitehead.

"William Kelly was a genius, not a businessman," she said.

In 1864, a Michigan mill made the first steel using Kelly's patented process, Whitehead said, adding that Kelly died in 1888 in Louisville. "When he was a frail old man near death, another famous steel man came to pay homage to him," she declared. "He was Andrew Carnegie."

Three historical markers in Lyon County commemorate "Crazy" Kelly. One, in Kuttawa, stands next to a surviving "Kelly Kettle." He sold many of the large iron containers to sugar producers in the Deep South.

Concluded Walker:

> *The genius of William Kelly…affects all our lives every day…William Kelly was not at the time of his work, nor since, been appreciated and recognized by…Lyon Countians…Kentucky or the world. I fear that sometimes we eat and drink of the labors of others and like the hog munching acorns under the oak tree, we never look up to see from whence it came.*

The Only Good Outlaw Is a Dead One

It was said that the mere mention of U.S. marshal E.D. Nix's name struck terror in the hearts of Oklahoma outlaws. "Sometimes I get a little suspicious of all

The Famous and Not So Famous

Marshall E.D. Nix's gravestone, Paducah.

the things that have been said or written about my uncle," admitted the late Herman Graham of Paducah, a Nix nephew. "But he was quite a man."

A Calloway County native, Nix moved to the Oklahoma Territory, where President Grover Cleveland named him marshal. At the end of Nix's three-year tenure, nine outlaws had been shot dead and forty-seven hanged, and more than five thousand other crooks were behind bars, according to *Oklahombres Revisited*, a book by Thomas R. Holland.

Holland was inspired by *Oklahombres: Particularly the Wilder Ones*, Nix's 1929 autobiography, which he co-authored with Gordon Hines. Holland also borrowed clippings and other firsthand accounts from Graham's scrapbook.

Nix and his deputies, including the celebrated "Three Guardsmen"—Bill Tilghman, Heck Thomas and Chris Masden—hunted down desperadoes like the Doolin-Dalton gang, which shot it out with peace officers in Ingalls, Oklahoma. Three deputies died in a hail of bullets, prompting Oklahoma's chief judge to wire Nix, "The only good outlaw is a dead one. I hope you will instruct your deputies to bring in dead outlaws in the future."

Jim Masterson, Bat's brother, was a Nix deputy. So was Tom Mix before he rode off into the sunset as a cowboy movie star.

The son of Simpson Socrates Nix, a Confederate army veteran, E.D. Nix was born near Coldwater in 1861, the year the Civil War began. He moved to Oklahoma in 1889, settling in Guthrie, the territorial capital.

Nix became a well-to-do business owner before he pinned on a badge in 1893. Nix was thirty-two, "the youngest man assigned to such a position," according to the online *Encyclopedia of Oklahoma History and Culture.*

On September 16, 1893, Nix's pistol shot opened the 5.6-million-acre Cherokee Strip to 100,000 settlers and speculators seeking free land. It was the largest land rush in American history.

Fifteen days before, Nix had fired his pistol in anger in a gunfight that went down in Sooner State history as the Battle of Ingalls. Almost two years afterward, Nix told his side of the story in a July 30, 1895 letter he wrote to U.S. attorney general Judson Harmon. Nix was responding to a claim for damages filed by a barkeep named Murray who was allegedly in cahoots with the outlaws.

In the letter, which is preserved at the National Archives in Washington, Nix explained:

> *One George Ransom owned a saloon in the town of Ingalls and this man Murray worked for him as bar tender. The outlaws Bill Doolan, "Bitter Creek," "Tulsa Jack," "Dynamite Dick," "Red Buck," Tom Jones and numerous others made this saloon their headquarters, and Ransom, Murray and other citizens catered to their trade, carried them news of the movements of the deputy Marshals, furnished them with ammunition, cared for their horses, permitted them to eat at their tables and sleep in their beds. These facts were well known to the community, although a conviction on the charge of harboring or aiding and abetting criminals against the laws of the United States could never be sustained, by reason of the fact that the entire community was under duress and would not testify for fear of losing their lives and property.*
>
> *On the 1st day of September 1893, a party of deputy marshals who had been sent after these outlaws by me, arrived in the vicinity of Ingalls, and the outlaws mentioned herein were at the time in the town and in the saloon of Rensom [sic], where this man Murray worked. As usual the outlaws had received notice of the proximity of the deputies and they sent a messenger to the deputies inviting them to come into the town if they thought they, the deputies, could take them. The deputies accepted the invitation and after posting their forces, sent a messenger to the outlaws with a request to surrender and were answered with Winchester shots.*

The Famous and Not So Famous

"Bitter Creek" ran out of the saloon in question and fired one shot towards the north where some of the deputies were stationed, and turning, received the fire of the deputies which burst the magazine of his [W]inchester and wounded him in the thigh. In the meantime, a heavy fire was directed at the deputies by the balance of the outlaws from the saloon building and the fire was returned by the deputies which literally riddled the saloon. A horse was killed by the deputies which was tied in front of the saloon... The fire of the deputies becoming too hot for the outlaws, they escaped out of a side door and took refuge in a large stable mentioned. This man Murray came to the front door of the saloon either just before the outlaws left the building or just after, it is not known which. However, when he first appeared in the door-way, he had the door open just a short distance and had his [W]inchester to his shoulder in the act of firing. This was previous to the deputies becoming aware of the fact of the outlaws having left the building. Three of the deputies seeing him in the position he was in, fired at him simultaneously. Two shots struck him in the ribs and one broke his arm in two places.

Eight or ten horses were killed and nine persons killed and wounded. One deputy was killed outright at the first fire and two more died the next day. Three outlaws were wounded and one captured. The one captured was afterwards sentenced to fifty years in the penitentiary and is now serving his time.

Very respectfully, E.D. Nix U.S. Marshal
Evitt Dumas Nix
United States Marshal 1893–1896

Nix raised a special unit of one hundred marshals to track down the gunmen who got away from Ingalls. Nix was gone by the time the officers were able to finish off the gang in 1898. Nix had been fired two years before.

"Critics charged that he mismanaged public funds, and an audit resulted in his dismissal," the encyclopedia says. "Many historians believe that Nix was a victim of the fee system used at that time for payment of U.S. Marshals Service officers." In any event, Nix claimed that while he was a marshal, "not a single man was killed who was not a notorious lawbreaker."

Wounded by train robbers in 1894, Nix narrowly escaped death many times. But one of his most famous encounters with crooks came long after his Oklahoma lawman days.

It was 1931. Nix, seventy, was a partner in a St. Louis brokerage company.

Two men walked in, pulled pistols and demanded cash. Nix calmly drew from his briefcase the old six-shooter he had taken from Bill Doolin. The would-be thieves ran away.

Nix fired at the fleeing crooks, but nobody got hurt. "My eye is bad," he told the newspapers. "I must be getting old. I tried to hit their legs, but I missed 'em."

Nix died in California in 1946. Cremated, his ashes were buried in Paducah's Oak Grove Cemetery beneath a small gray tombstone that identified him as "First U.S. Marshal Oklahoma Territory."

In *Oklahombres*, Hines wrote of Nix:

> He was a quiet, unassuming business man with none of the bombast of the early day politicians with no political aspirations, who only wished to rear his family and conduct his business in peace. His community drafted him into service and pulled the necessary wires to get the appointment, not because they wanted to give him a political sinecure, but because their homes and their lives were at stake and E.D. Nix seemed to be the man who could make this part of Oklahoma Territory safe for respectable people.

Hines concluded, "He *was* the man, and he *did* the job."

Was the Mother of Mother's Day from Henderson?

Henderson schoolteacher Mary Towles Sasseen Wilson loved her mother so much that she began a one-woman crusade for a national holiday honoring all mothers. Hence, some people in Henderson claim that she was the real mother of Mother's Day.

But about the only thing connecting Wilson to the Henderson County seat is an old black-and-white state historical society marker. The weather-beaten metal plaque claims that Wilson first celebrated Mother's Day with her pupils in 1887.

Even so, most history books say that Anna M. Jarvis of Philadelphia started Mother's Day. She convinced Congress to declare a Mother's Day holiday in 1914.

But Wilson wrote a pamphlet in 1893 that suggested ways for teachers to celebrate Mother's Day with their students. The county library has a rare copy of the booklet in which Wilson proposed a national Mother's Day so that "much of the veneration, love and respect due to parents might, by song, verse and story, be inculcated in the next generation."

Wilson wanted April 20 to be Mother's Day because it was her mother's birthday. Congress named Mother's Day the second Sunday in May.

Files in the local library bulge with yellowing newspaper clippings that seem to support the claim that Mother's Day was Wilson's idea. An old issue of the *Milwaukee Journal* says that the western Kentucky teacher "traveled extensively and addressed educational societies and other organizations in various parts of the country in her effort to have the observance of Mother's Day nationally recognized and adopted."

In 1899, Wilson ran unsuccessfully for the Democratic nomination for superintendent of public instruction. The *Louisville Courier-Journal* described her as "the author and originator of Mother's Day."

The paper said that the candidate already had convinced many school officials in other states and cities, such as Boston and Brooklyn, to celebrate Mother's Day. "The effect on character must be for good and does credit to both heart and head of the originator," the newspaper declared.

Born in 1860, Mary Towles Sasseen grew up dreaming of becoming a mother herself. The tall, red-haired woman was forty-four when she fell in love with Judge Marshall Wilson. They married and moved to Pensacola, Florida, in hopes of improving Mary's poor health.

The marriage lasted only eighteen months. She died in childbirth. The baby also died.

Wilson perished just two days before her mother's birthday in 1906. She was buried in Pensacola.

In her booklet, Wilson wrote:

> *We find that every man and woman, whom the world has called great, whose words have been treasured for their wisdom and goodness, all cherished their memories of mother, of happy, innocent childhood and of home; their testimony is always interesting, always beautiful, and they speak of the common sentiment of the human race. The love of home is universal, but often times the appreciation of the mother comes only after an irretrievable loss.*

"After the Manner of the Booker T. Washington School in Alabama"

Reverend Dennis Henry Anderson lifted up his prayers with a pick and shovel. A son of slaves, he asked God to give him strength to train African

Above: Reverend Anderson dug the foundations for the first building at West Kentucky Industrial College. *Courtesy of the West Kentucky Community and Technical College Archives.*

Left: Reverend Dennis Henry Anderson. *Courtesy of the West Kentucky Community and Technical College Archives.*

American teachers in Jim Crow Paducah. He dug the foundation for the first building himself.

"It was back in 1909 when African Americans couldn't go to white colleges," said author Janett Blythe. "The only teacher training facility for African Americans in Kentucky was in Frankfort at what is now Kentucky State University."

Anderson's school, West Kentucky Industrial College, eventually became West Kentucky Technical College. It merged with 1932-vintage Paducah Community College in 2003 to form West Kentucky Community and Technical College.

The Famous and Not So Famous

Monument to the Andersons outside the Anderson Building on the WKCTC campus.

Blythe is director of public relations and marketing at WKCTC. She wrote *My West Kentucky*, the first history book about the college Anderson started, and *Upward Stride*, a history of WKCTC.

When Anderson began his college, segregation and race discrimination were the law and the social order in Paducah. White mobs lynched at least four local black men in the 1900s.

Anderson's faith fired him, Blythe said. He was a Methodist minister.

Anderson said his inspiration was Booker T. Washington, who founded Tuskegee Institute in Alabama in 1881. Both men, Blythe said, "believed that education and training were catalysts for changing things for the better."

Though a pioneer African American educator in western Kentucky, Anderson was born in Jackson, in western Tennessee, in 1866—a year after the end of the Civil War and slavery. Educated at historically black Lane College in Jackson, Anderson eventually settled in Paducah, where he preached in local churches and taught African American pupils in a one-room log schoolhouse.

"But he soon aspired for more," Blythe said.

Anderson's wife, Artelia, was also a teacher. She helped him start his school.

Sometimes, the couple worked late into the night. While he muscled a pick and shovel, she held a lantern, Blythe said. Anderson said he built the school "out of logs and faith."

Anderson also went door to door seeking contributions. People chipped in nickels, dimes and even pennies. Artelia Anderson donated her salary of fifty-five dollars a month, and the city government furnished a few hundred dollars, according to Blythe.

Anderson laid the cornerstone for the school in 1911, but he believed he needed state support to succeed. Thus began his seven-year campaign for state funding.

He made four trips to faraway Frankfort—the second time astride a motorcycle—before money was forthcoming. The motorcycle journey, in 1914, was the hardest. Ku Klux Klansmen chased Anderson and his bike into a swamp. He escaped them but later hit a bump in a rocky road, flew over the handlebars of his motorcycle and broke his shoulder.

Undaunted, he nursed his battered bike to Frankfort, where "his arm in a sling he again appealed to the General Assembly for money to start his college," Blythe said. Not until 1918 did Governor A.O. Stanley sign into law a bill creating a junior college in Paducah for African Americans, "after the manner of the Booker T. Washington School in Alabama."

Through the years, enrollment and state funding increased. More buildings went up. "The school even had dormitories, and people came to the school from all over the country," Blythe said.

In 1938, the state legislature turned the Frankfort-based State Normal School for Colored Persons into Kentucky State College for Negroes.

Lawmakers also merged West Kentucky Industrial College into the new four-year school and shifted the teacher-training program in Paducah to Frankfort. At the same time, Anderson stepped down as president of West Kentucky Industrial College, which closed and reopened as West Kentucky State Vocational School.

For many years, the school was a focus of pride in Paducah's African American community, Blythe said. "It was more than a school. There were all sorts of community programs and events at West Kentucky. It was a wonderful place to go for fellowship."

In 1979, the state shifted the school from downtown to a new building and a new campus next to Paducah Community College just west of the city. The name was changed to West Kentucky State Vocational-Technical School.

The move sparked controversy. "Many African Americans felt they had been robbed of what was their school in their community," Blythe said.

The school became West Kentucky Technical College in 1998. Four years before, the school building had been named for Anderson.

Out front is a shiny black marble memorial to the Andersons. Artelia Anderson died in 1936, and her husband followed in 1952.

Blythe thinks the founder of old West Kentucky Industrial College would be proud of WKCTC. "He believed in educating people," she said. "I don't believe the form would matter to him."

"We Were the United Auto Workers, and We Felt Like We Were Doing Right"

Ermon Harp left her native western Kentucky looking for work, not a place in American labor history. She found both in Detroit, where she worked in a factory and joined one of the first sit-down strikes. The year was 1937.

"They called us Communists—and just about everything else you could think of," said Harp. "But it didn't bother me a particle. We were the United Auto Workers, and we felt like we were doing right."

She felt that way until she died at age ninety-seven in 1992.

To the end, independence and self-reliance characterized the little grandmother with turquoise-blue eyes and soft white hair. She got herself to the First Presbyterian Church. Her daughter and son-in-law lived in town, but Harp would not allow either of them to take her to Sunday services. She called a cab.

Ermon Harp and her husband, Lube, were part of a mass migration of Kentuckians to Detroit seeking work in the auto industry in the 1920s. The Harps left Milburn, in Carlisle County, in 1922, after struggling to make ends meet on a hardscrabble farm.

Fifteen years later, she helped make union history. Was she scared when she joined the strike?

"Goodness, no," she said. "There was nothing to be scared of."

There was, of course. UAW organizers and members were fired, blacklisted and even assaulted.

The year Harp struck, Ford Motor Company guards severely beat union activists, including Walter Reuther, the UAW's president and guiding spirit for many years.

Historians credit the sit-down strike with helping pave the way for union organizing in American industry. The most significant sit-down strike began on December 30, 1936, at the General Motors plant in Flint, Michigan, near Detroit. In January, police stormed the plant. Workers repelled them and held on until February 11, 1937, when GM recognized the UAW.

The Flint sit-down "was the most pivotal strike in early UAW history," according to the union. "It established the UAW as the sole bargaining representative for workers at the world's largest corporation and set the stage for organizing industrial workers across the United States."

Harp's strike came soon after the Flint sit-down. "I had no idea that what I was doing was making history," she said.

Lube and Ermon Harp and their daughter, Elaine, at their Detroit home. *Courtesy of Nancy Turner.*

Harp had a head full of memories about UAW organizing drives. "Our people were getting beat up all over town. But nobody got hurt where I worked. I guess it was because it was a small plant."

Harp sat down on strike at the Advance Stamping Company. She was working on an assembly line, fitting together distributors for car engines.

Fifteen women and forty-eight men stopped working at their machines and wouldn't budge. "It all went off smooth as you please," she said. "There was no rough stuff."

"People brought us hot food, blankets and pillows. We organized a square dance. Some of the men played cards, and we turned the radio on to a church service on Sunday."

Harp saw her spouse during the day, but the strikers stayed in the plant. "We found some big barrels, put some boards over them, spread down our blankets and slept pretty well," she said.

At about the same time of Ermon's sit-down strike, Lube Harp joined the UAW at a General Motors factory where he worked. Harp said she became "union all the way" at the plant where she worked before landing a job at Advance Stamping.

"I'd worked there eleven years when the boss came in one day and said, 'Ermon, come pick up your check. You're through,'" Harp remembered. "Later, I found out he'd given my job to his girlfriend. That's why I went union and why Detroit went union. It was because of things like that that weren't fair."

A Man of Courage

Lela Scopes remembered what her brother told her after he landed a teaching job in Dayton, Tennessee, in 1924: "I'm going there because it's a small town with a small school where I won't get in any deep water."

In 1925, Paducah-born John Thomas Scopes became known worldwide when he was convicted of teaching evolution in what went down in history as "the Monkey Trial." The trial inspired the play and movie *Inherit the Wind*.

"The cause defended at Dayton is a continuing one that has existed throughout man's brief history and will continue as long as man is here," Scopes wrote in *Center of the Storm*, his 1967 memoirs. "It is the cause of freedom, for which man must do what he can."

Scopes generally shunned the limelight after his trial, one of the most famous courtroom battles in American history. He spent the rest of his life working quietly as a geologist, some of the time in South America.

John T. Scopes. *Courtesy of the Library of Congress.*

Scopes tombstone, Paducah.

Scopes died in 1970 at age seventy and was buried on the family plot in Oak Grove Cemetery in his hometown. A state historical society marker at the cemetery entrance tells about him and the trial, during which he spoke not a word.

"I did little more than sit, proxylike, in freedom's chair that hot, unforgettable summer—no great feat, despite the notoriety it has brought me," he explained in his reminiscences, which he co-authored with James Presley. "My role was a passive one that developed out of my willingness to test what I considered a bad law."

Scopes meant the Butler Act. The measure forbade the teaching of evolution in Tennessee's public schools.

The New York–based American Civil Liberties Union said the law was unconstitutional. The group bought ads in Volunteer State newspapers offering to defend, free of charge, any teacher who taught evolution.

After spying one of the ads in a Chattanooga newspaper, some Dayton businessmen asked Scopes to stand trial. They figured the publicity would put tiny Dayton, the seat of Rhea County in southeastern Tennessee, on the map.

The Famous and Not So Famous

School was out for the summer, but Scopes, twenty-four, said he had taught evolution. He said he believed in evolution as "the only plausible explanation of man's long and torturous journey to his present physical and mental development."

The Kentuckian agreed to stand trial on principle.

He was charged with willfully teaching "a certain theory or theories that denied the story of the divine creation of man as taught in the Bible, but did teach instead thereof, that man is descended from a lower order of animals...against the peace and dignity of the State."

Scopes was freed on bond pending his trial, which was set for July.

The trial was more than the *State of Tennessee v. John T. Scopes*. It was a clash of American values—the newfangled urban science and modernism versus rural, old-time Protestant fundamentalist Christianity. "Modernists exhibited little understanding of religion and fundamentalists showed scant appreciation for science," said Dr. David Krueger, a retired history professor at West Kentucky Community and Technical College in Paducah.

The attorneys represented both sides of the sharp divide. Tennessee summoned William Jennings Bryan of Nebraska as special prosecutor. Bryan was a devout Christian and a stubborn foe of evolution. He was also an accomplished orator, former U.S. senator, secretary of state and three-time Democratic presidential candidate.

The ACLU hired Clarence Darrow to lead Scopes's defense team. Many people considered Darrow the country's top defense lawyer. He was from Chicago, believed in evolution and was agnostic.

Scopes and Bryan had crossed paths. The Scopes family moved from Paducah to Illinois and lived for a time in Salem, where Bryan grew up. Bryan was the commencement speaker when Scopes graduated from the local high school. They met at a pretrial banquet.

"John, I know you," Bryan amiably told Scopes. "I think you're one of those high school students who made a disturbance at that commencement address I delivered in Salem several years ago!"

Scopes said he "grinned, and possibly blushed, impressed that [Bryan] remembered."

He added that Bryan said there was no reason he and Scopes should not be friends. "I agreed; I told him I respected him despite our differences of opinion. 'Good,' he said; 'we shall get along fine.' He was in a fine mood and we had a pleasant dinner."

The trial was not pleasant. Bryan and Darrow dueled in the sweltering Tennessee summer like gladiators. The courtroom became so hot that the trial was moved outdoors to the tree-shaded courthouse lawn.

The trial lasted eight days, ending on July 21 in a not unexpected guilty verdict. After the judge fined Scopes $100, one of his lawyers reminded the judge that he had not permitted the defendant to speak before punishment was meted out.

Scopes finally got his say:

> *Your Honor, I feel that I have been convicted of violating an unjust statute. I will continue in the future, as I have in the past, to oppose this law in any way I can. Any other action would be in violation of my ideals of academic freedom, that is to teach the truth as guaranteed in our Constitution, of personal and religious freedom. I think the fine is unjust.*

Unmoved, the judge again fined Scopes $100, which the ACLU paid. He left the courtroom and teaching.

Meanwhile, the ACLU appealed to the Tennessee Supreme Court. The justices ruled that the Butler Act was constitutional but set aside the fine on the grounds that the jury, not the judge, should have fixed Scopes's punishment. Not until 1967 did the Tennessee legislature repeal the Butler Act.

The Scopes trial, covered live by WGN radio of Chicago, did put Dayton on the map, but not in the way the town boosters intended. Big city newspaper reporters, notably H.L. Mencken of the *Baltimore Sun*, wrote stories ridiculing the locals.

Dayton became a virtual circus with vendors hawking hot dogs, lemonade and books on biology and religion, Scopes wrote. "The Anti-Evolution league set up headquarters downtown, and sold books and pamphlets, including T.T. Martin's *Hell and the High Schools*. Martin was the league's secretary. Everybody was doing business."

Scopes added:

> *From the beginning to the end of the test case Ringling Brothers or Barnum and Bailey would have been pressed hard to produce more acts and sideshows and freaks than Dayton had. The curious of all complexions and descriptions and persuasions poured in to become a part of the drama that H.L. Mencken had christened the Monkey Trial. A showman like P.T. Barnum would have gloated over the possibilities that Dayton offered and called it a natural.*

Lela Scopes said their father, English-born Thomas Scopes, traveled to Dayton to be with John. Scopes said his father was his lifelong inspiration.

The Famous and Not So Famous

After he became an American citizen, the elder Scopes embraced socialism, became a labor union activist and was "a stanch fighter for workingmen's rights through the rest of his active years," according to his son.

Thomas Scopes was also a teetotaler, according to his daughter. "After the trial, Mr. Darrow would give us a bottle of wine every Christmas," she said. The bottles would go into the pantry, unopened. They stayed corked until Thomas Scopes died in 1946, or so the children thought.

After their father was gone, John suggested they uncork one of the bottles, Lela said. "We did and every one of them was filled with water. Our housekeeper had been secretly drinking the wine all along."

Her brother was a prelaw major at the University of Kentucky, where he graduated in 1924. Following the trial, he accepted a scholarship to study geology at the University of Chicago. Geology became his life's calling.

He worked as a geologist for oil companies in Venezuela, Texas and Arkansas before he retired in 1963. He met his wife, a South Carolinian and a Catholic, in Venezuela. They were married in her church; Scopes was baptized a Catholic. "News stories subsequently made a point of my being a member of the Catholic Church," he wrote. "I emphasized to all who interviewed me that I had done this simply to please my bride."

There are no religious words carved on his simple gray tombstone. "A man of courage" is his epitaph.

HE WAS CERTAINLY A GRAND MUSICIAN

Riverboat orchestra leader Fate Marable is not as famous as the teenage trumpet player he recruited in 1919.

"He hired Louis Armstrong," said Dr. Tammy Turner, a music professor and author in Paducah, Marable's hometown. Marable signed up Armstrong, age eighteen, after "developing a fascination with the New Orleans style of jazz, a rich, vibrant music forged from a mixture of West African and European musical traditions."

Marable was more succinct. He said jazz "just got under my skin."

The piano got under Marable's skin when he was a kid. His mother disapproved, according to Turner, who teaches jazz history at West Kentucky Community and Technical College and at nearby Murray State University. "She was a trained pianist who initially refused to allow him to play the piano. He would practice when she was away from the house until she overheard his playing and finally acquiesced to his request for instruction."

Above: Fate Marable, at the piano, and his band aboard the SS *Capitol*. *Courtesy of the Jazz Archive, Tulane University.*

Below: Marable's grave, Paducah.

The Famous and Not So Famous

Hotel Metropolitan, Paducah.

Marable, who was African American like Armstrong, grew up in a Jim Crow Paducah when segregation and race discrimination were the rule. In 1907, he decided to start a piano career elsewhere—on the Mississippi River. He was seventeen.

"Marable was hired by Captain Joseph Streckfus, general manager of Streckfus Steamers, to perform on the steamboat *J.S. No. 1*," Turner said. "The Streckfus Company owned a line of excursion boats that traveled the Mississippi from New Orleans to Minneapolis, entertaining patrons with music and dancing during the trip."

At first, Marable and a violinist were the only professional music makers in the boat's crew. "But as time passed, other musicians were added to form a small group," Turner said. "Marable became their band leader."

She added:

> *Streckfus had distinct musical tastes and ideas which were shared by Marable. For this reason, he was allowed far greater musical freedom than his predecessors. Streckfus trusted him and gave him considerable control in the hiring of new musicians. In 1917, Marable assembled his first band, the Kentucky Jazz Band, so named because all the members were from Paducah.*

Marable enlisted talented musicians, Turner said. But the more jazz Marable heard on stops in the Crescent City, the less he liked the music his band was playing.

So he started employing jazz players from New Orleans. "Some of the musicians were hired in late 1918, with several others joining the ensemble by 1919," Turner said.

Marable's band grew into an orchestra. In his 1954 autobiography *Satchmo: My Life in New Orleans*, Armstrong said he joined Marable and his musicians aboard the steamer *Sydney*:

> *He was a great piano man and he also played the calliope on the top deck of the* Sydney. *Just before the boat left the docks for one of its moonlight trips up the Mississippi, Fate would sit down at this calliope and damn near play the keys off of it. He was certainly a grand musician.*

Armstrong, who had been a star in Kid Ory's band, said he jumped at the opportunity to play for Marable:

> *It meant a great advancement in my musical career because his musicians had to read music perfectly. Ory's men did not. Later on I found out that Fate Marable had just as many jazz greats as Kid Ory, and they were better men besides because they could read music and they could improvise. Fate's had a wide range and they played all the latest music because they could read at sight. Kid Ory's band could catch on to a tune quickly, and once they had it no one could outplay them. But I wanted to do more than fake the music all the time because there is more to music than just playing one style.*

Marable also signed on siblings who became famous jazz musicians: drummer Warren "Baby" Dodds and clarinetist Johnny Dodds. "In less than two years, Marable's orchestra was considered one of the finest dance bands in the United States," Turner said.

Being able to read music was not a prerequisite to playing New Orleans–style jazz, according to Turner. "But it was a part of the foundation on which Marable built his ensemble. As an accomplished musician, he demanded rigorous musicianship of those who worked with him. Daily rehearsals lasted an average of one to two hours."

Musicians joked that Marable was running a "floating conservatory." Armstrong remembered that Marable "had his own way of dealing with musicians." He explained:

The Famous and Not So Famous

If one of us made an error or played part of a piece wrong he would not say a thing about it until everyone thought it had been forgotten. When you came to work the next day with a bad hangover from the night before, he picked up the music you had failed with and asked you to play it before the other members of the band. And believe me brother it was no fun being shown up before all the other fellows if you did not play the passage right; we used to call this experience our Waterloo. This was Fate's way of making his men rest properly so they could work perfectly on the job the next night. I learned something from that, and to this day I think it is good psychology.

When Marable put Armstrong on the payroll, he knew his new trumpet player had never been far from New Orleans. Armstrong said Marable's older musicians warned him "Little Louis" would never leave town. "But Fate had a way of his own," Armstrong wrote.

He could see that I was very happy in his wonderful orchestra, playing the kind of music I had never played before in my life and piling up all of the experiences I had dreamed of as an ambitious kid. He made me a feature man in his orchestra. I can still hear that fine applause I got from the customers.

Turner said Marable's musicians indeed played more than jazz. "Orchestra members invariably became educated in a wide variety of styles. Occasionally, a musician lacking strong music reading or technical skills would be hired if Marable believed he had great potential. Louis Armstrong is the most noteworthy example, for his music reading skills were poor when he joined the orchestra." Armstrong said Marable "knew all this when he hired me, but he liked my tone and the way I could catch on. That was enough for him. Being a grand and experienced musician, he knew that just being around musicians who read music I would automatically learn myself. Within no time at all I was reading everything he put before me."

Through the years, several other jazz greats came through Marable's "conservatory." "In 1921, Johnny Dodds relocated to Chicago to join famed New Orleans trumpeter and bandleader Joe 'King' Oliver," Turner said. "Less than a year later, 'Baby' Dodds, banjoist and guitarist Johnny St. Cyr and Armstrong followed. They were added to Oliver's ensemble."

By the mid-1920s, Armstrong had started his own jazz band. He was billed as "the World's Greatest Trumpet Player," Turner said.

Meanwhile, Marable encouraged Armstrong and other African American bandleaders and musicians to play in Paducah. But while African American musicians performed for whites at hotels like the Irvin Cobb, they could not stay in them.

Most of the bands slept at the African American–owned Hotel Metropolitan. The old two-story wooden lodgings are preserved as a museum and operated by the nonprofit Upper Town Heritage Foundation.

"Fate Marable was born and lived just around the corner from the hotel," said Betty Dobson, who helped start the foundation. "Besides Louis Armstrong, Baby Dodds, Cab Calloway, Count Basie, Duke Ellington and Ella Fitzgerald all stayed here. The jam sessions that followed their performances were amazing."

Dobson said that Armstrong reportedly refused to play his trumpet unless Velma Hamock would sing along. Hamock and her husband owned a funeral home in Paducah for many years.

Besides the Dodds brothers and Armstrong, others left Marable to start their own renowned jazz bands, Turner said. "Some of these included saxophonist Earl Carruthers, who joined Jimmie Lunceford's band in the early 1920s; saxophonist Tab Smith, who was recruited by Count Basie in 1935; and outstanding bassist Jimmy Blanton, who joined Duke Ellington's Orchestra in 1939."

The next year, Marable went ashore for good in St. Louis, where he played in nightclubs. He was fifty-six when he died of pneumonia in 1947. He was buried in Paducah's Oak Grove Cemetery, where an upright piano is carved on his tombstone.

"There Is a Real *X-Files* Twist to This"

Nobody knows what Captain Thomas F. Mantell Jr. was chasing through the winter sky on January 7, 1948. His pursuit of the "flying saucer" cost him his life. The twenty-five-year-old Kentucky Air National Guard pilot from Louisville died in the crash of his P-51 Mustang fighter plane near Franklin, the Simpson County seat.

A county historical marker just off Interstate 65 in Franklin commemorates the aviator's death. "Because he was killed trying to catch an unidentified flying object, the story made headlines around the world," said John Trowbridge, command historian of the Kentucky National Guard. "There is a real *X-Files* twist to this, too. Mantell lived almost his entire life in

The Famous and Not So Famous

Above: Mantell marker near Franklin.

Left: Mantell tombstone, Zachary Taylor National Cemetery, Louisville.

Louisville. But he was born in a hospital in Franklin, only a few miles from where he was killed."

A World War II hero, Mantell is buried in Zachary Taylor National Cemetery in Louisville. The Louisville Male High School graduate is probably all but forgotten, except to family members and friends, Trowbridge said.

"But the investigation of Mantell's crash became part of Project Sign," Trowbridge added. "Project Sign later became Project Blue Book, the Air Force's official investigation into UFOs."

Mantell and three other pilots, also in single-seat P-51s, were flying near Fort Knox when their radios crackled with a strange request from the control tower at nearby Godman Field. "They were asked to investigate an unidentified flying object which had been seen in the area," Trowbridge said. Colonel Guy F. Hicks, Godman Field commander, "said he observed the flying saucer for some time," according to an Associated Press story at the time.

One of the warplanes, evidently low on fuel, flew on to Louisville. Hicks said in the news account that the air base lost contact with the other three fighters "in about 20 minutes. Two of the planes later called back and reported no success."

The other P-51 was Mantell's. His fighter was not equipped with oxygen for high-altitude flight, Trowbridge said, adding, "He apparently flew too high, blacked out and crashed."

Glenn Mayes, who lived near Franklin, claimed "he saw Mantell's plane flying at an extremely high altitude shortly before it apparently exploded in the air," the AP story said. "The plane circled three times like the pilot didn't know where he was going, and then started into a dive from about 20,000 feet," Mayes said. "About halfway down there was a terrific explosion."

The wreckage of Mantell's doomed plane was "scattered over an area two miles wide," according to Mayes. "None of the craft burned," he said.

Many aviation historians say the speedy, machine gun–armed Mustang was the best propeller-driven fighter of World War II. Mantell, who joined the Army Air Force in 1942, piloted troop transport planes in the global conflict.

"He participated in the Normandy invasion and many other European operations," according to the AP account. He earned a Distinguished Flying Cross and four Air Medals for bravery, according to the Kentucky Air Guard.

Many people apparently saw the "saucer," including "several other pilots" who flew after it, the story at the time of the crash said. Two of the aviators, James Garret and William Crenshaw, both from Hopkinsville, thought the UFO was a balloon. "Astronomers at Vanderbilt University, Nashville,

Tenn., reported they saw some object in the sky…which they believed to be a balloon but the Nashville Weather Bureau said it knew of no balloons in that vicinity," the AP story said.

In Ohio, "a flaming red cone" was reportedly spotted close to the air base at Wilmington. "Army spokesmen said they had no information on the object or its origin," the AP story said.

It was suggested that the UFO was a huge navy "Skyhook" balloon. "Whatever it was, it gave Capt. Tom Mantell his fifteen minutes of fame," said Trowbridge, who helped get the marker for Mantell in Franklin. The blue and gold plaque stands outside the Simpson County tourist office.

"It Was Something Beyond Prizes"

Ellis Wilson's art was exhibited in the Smithsonian Institution and at the New York World's Fair. "He is in almost every book about African American artists," said Dr. Steven Jones, chair of the Murray State University Department of Social Work, Criminal Justice and Gerontology.

Ellis Wilson. *Courtesy of Collins Wilson.*

But the art show that made Wilson proudest was a modest exhibit in Mayfield, his hometown, in 1947. "He said it was 'for all the folks to see,'" explained Jones, who lives in Mayfield.

When Wilson died in New York in 1977, he was all but unknown in Mayfield, where he was born in 1899. His old wood-frame house still stands on East Water Street. "There ought to at least be a state historical society marker honoring him at the house or at the courthouse," Jones said.

In the centennial year of Wilson's birth, Jones and Eva King, a Murray artist, decided Wilson merited more

Ellis Wilson and his home in Mayfield. *Courtesy of Eduardo Oronia.*

recognition locally. So did Albert Sperath, director of the Clara Eagle Art Gallery at Murray State University.

So in 2000, Wilson's works were exhibited at the Eagle Gallery and the Mayfield–Graves County Art Guild. From western Kentucky, Wilson's artwork migrated to the University of Kentucky in Lexington for another exhibition.

For the artist, more statewide recognition followed. Also in 2000, Kentucky Educational Television broadcast *Ellis Wilson—So Much to Paint*, a documentary program.

"The critics of Ellis Wilson's day described him as 'an interpreter of Negro life,'" King said. "He turned the everyday lives of black people into colorful, vibrant art. His paintings speak of family and community, of dignity and hard work and of joy and celebration."

As a young man, Wilson left Mayfield to study art in Chicago. But he mainly painted in New York City, where he lived for forty-nine years.

Racism stung Wilson for most of his life. Segregation and discrimination were the law in Mayfield and the social order elsewhere in America, including Chicago and New York.

Wilson got his big break in the 1940s, when he earned a pair of Guggenheim fellowships to travel and paint in the rural South. In the 1950s, he painted in Haiti. That artwork earned him more critical acclaim.

Even so, "the exhibition he regarded as one of the high points of his life was a small show in the library in Mayfield," wrote Romare Bearden and Harry Henderson in their book, *A History of African-American Artists from 1792 to the Present*. The authors devoted a chapter to Wilson.

"That he was so honored in the town where, as a child, he was told to get off the sidewalks and let the white people pass created his deepest satisfaction," Bearden and Henderson wrote. "It was something beyond prizes."

A copy of *Haitian Funeral Procession*, Wilson's most popular painting, hangs in the living room of Jones's house. Tulane University in New Orleans owns the original.

Viewers of the old *Cosby Show* probably would recognize the artwork. The set of the popular TV comedy series featured a print of *Haitian Funeral Procession*. "In an episode, Claire Huxtable [the wife of Dr. Cliff Huxtable, the character played by Bill Cosby] buys it at an auction," King said. "Claire says her uncle—she calls him Ellis Wilson—painted it, and she always wanted it. The picture continued to hang on the set, above the fireplace, during following episodes of the show."

An original Wilson painting—*Machine Shop*—hung in President Barack Obama's private senate office from 2005 to 2008. Soon after he was elected, Obama asked galleries to loan him important works of art connected with Illinois.

Wilson grew up in a Jim Crow Mayfield where the color line was rigid. African Americans were kept separate and unequal from whites. Local white mobs lynched at least four black men in the 1890s. In 1896, rampaging whites shot and killed three African Americans. The *New York Times* reported the shootings as "Race War in Mayfield, Ky."

Wilson's parents, Frank and Minnie Wilson, had six children. The family worshipped at Second Christian Church, which Minnie Wilson helped found on East Water Street, close to their home.

Ellis Wilson may have inherited his artistic talent from his father. A barber, the elder Wilson was also an amateur painter, according to King.

The family especially prized a pair of Frank Wilson's paintings. "If they would be around today, they would be considered primitives," Ellis Wilson told Henderson in a 1975 interview.

As a youngster, Wilson painted and drew when he could. He went to the Mayfield Colored Graded School on South Second Street, which survives as a private home.

Wilson had to work after school to help the family make ends meet, so he took a job as a window cleaner at the S.T. Day Ready-to-Wear Store. Bearden and Henderson wrote that "while...washing a...window, he drew a portrait with soap on it, immediately attracting a crowd. The delighted proprietor had him leave the portrait on the window and create a new one each week."

Wilson went as far in school as he could in Mayfield. He was barred from white-only Mayfield High School; all-black Dunbar High School had yet to be built.

"So Ellis Wilson did what a lot of blacks had to do in small Kentucky towns when they wanted to further their education back then," Jones said. "He went to what is now Kentucky State University in Frankfort, which had a high school department."

In 1917, Wilson traveled to the state capital and enrolled in the Kentucky Normal and Industrial Institute for Colored Persons, then the only Kentucky college open to African Americans. The teen was disappointed that the school had no art department. In 1919, he moved to Chicago to study at the prestigious Art Institute.

King said that Wilson became "part of the Great Migration which saw hundreds of thousands of blacks moving from the South to the North seeking jobs and educational opportunities." When he reached the Windy City, Wilson probably thought he had escaped the racial prejudice and anti-black violence of Kentucky. Then Chicago erupted in the bloodiest race riot in American history.

"I couldn't go downtown to the Art Institute," Wilson told Henderson. "They were shooting and carrying on."

Violence lasted for two weeks; thirty-eight people were killed, five hundred were injured and the homes of one thousand African Americans were burned. The riot started after enraged whites stoned to death a black youth who swam into a beach area on Lake Michigan informally reserved for whites.

After peace was restored, Wilson enthusiastically took up his studies. "They were good times," he recalled. "I had never been in a group of artists—you know, creative black people."

He finished at the Art Institute in 1923 and tried to make a living as a commercial artist in Chicago. But in 1928, he moved to New York. "Ellis Wilson arrived in Harlem—and found himself in the middle of a vibrant African American community that was almost bursting at the seams with artistic and cultural creativity," King said.

A year later, the stock market crashed, and the Great Depression hit. Times were hard; jobs were scarce. Finally, in 1935, Wilson got steady work with the Works Progress Administration. A centerpiece of President Franklin D.

The Famous and Not So Famous

Roosevelt's New Deal program for fighting the Depression, the WPA provided jobs for tens of thousands of out-of-work Americans, including artists.

In the WPA, Wilson got to know other African American artists. "It was really stimulating. It really got me to painting on my own," he told Henderson.

Again, Wilson faced racial injustice in a northern city. "Segregation ruled in the art world just as it did the rest of American society," King said. "Wilson and his fellow black artists were barred from most white-owned galleries. They had a hard time finding places to show their work. Their exhibitions were limited to places like public libraries, the 'colored' branches of the YMCA, and the homes of African Americans who had some money."

Wilson persisted and managed to get his work displayed in some city art galleries and at the 1939 World's Fair. He applied for a Guggenheim fellowship in 1939, explaining, "Practically all of my life I have been painting under difficult conditions...I want to paint all the time—everything of interest and beauty."

Wilson was rejected. He was turned down again in 1940 and 1941. Wilson wouldn't give up, and finally he won Guggenheims in 1944 and 1945. Wilson caught the attention of art critic Justus Bier, who "understood what a persistent effort a poor Kentucky black youth had had to make to win a Guggenheim fellowship," Bearden and Henderson wrote.

Favorable reviews from Bier and other critics got Wilson more exhibitions in museums and galleries, including the Smithsonian Institution in Washington, D.C., and the J.B. Speed Museum in Louisville. Wilson traveled and painted widely. He visited Mayfield and painted farmhands working in a tobacco patch, clay mineworkers and the locally famous Wooldridge Monuments, according to King. Wilson told Henderson that the strange stone statuary in Maplewood Cemetery had "scared the britches off" him as a child.

"Although he was not an artistic innovator, his paintings changed perceptions of black people wherever they were shown," Bearden and Henderson wrote. "Millions of Americans have seen them on Bill Cosby's television shows."

In 1947, considerably fewer people saw Wilson's little art show at the Graves County Public Library. No matter, Wilson was delighted, Jones said.

"About 30 years ago," the *Mayfield News Graphic* reported, "a little Negro boy used to deliver packages for the old S.T. Day Ready-to-Wear Store. Now that little boy is back in his home town with an exhibit of his paintings. He is Ellis Wilson, one of the country's leading Negro Artists today."

Wilson never made much money as an artist, Jones said. When he died, he was buried in an unmarked pauper's grave in New York. The location is unknown, King added.

"Wilson strongly believed that the work of black artists deserved just as much respect as the work of white artists, but he was not politically active about it," King said. "He was a quiet, shy man who preferred to let his art speak for him. It did eloquently, and continues to do so."

"A Union Card in One Hand and an NAACP Card in the Other"

When W.C. Young died in Paducah, he was living next door to his church and down the street from his last union office. The symbolism wasn't lost on the national labor and civil rights leader and the man for whom the city's W.C. Young Community Center is named. The community center is the headquarters for Paducah's annual Eighth of August Celebration, a traditional African American homecoming and holiday.

"I really believed what I was taught in Sunday school," said Young, who died in 1996 at age seventy-seven. "You are supposed to love your brother and sister. That's the way it is with the union movement."

Young founded the community center in 1976. Named for him later, the center has become the headquarters for the annual Eighth of August Celebration, a traditionally African American holiday in the city that began many years ago.

Born in Paducah in 1919, Young was baptized into

W.C. Young. *Courtesy of the Western Kentucky AFL-CIO Area Council.*

The Famous and Not So Famous

Washington Street Baptist Church in 1937, the fateful year in which Paducah had its own version of the biblical flood. Young ended up a deacon, trustee, moderator, Sunday school superintendent and building committee chairman.

Young also spent forty-six years in the labor movement. He retired in 1987 as Region 10 director of the AFL-CIO's Committee on Political Education.

Young pocketed his first union card in 1941 as a member of the Brotherhood of Railway Clerks at Paducah's old Illinois Central Railroad repair shops. Those were Jim Crow days in Paducah. The majority white society kept African Americans separate and unequal.

But Young lived to see organized labor make common cause with the civil rights movement. J.W. Cleary, a former president of the Paducah–McCracken County NAACP branch and a member of United Steelworkers Local 550 at the Paducah gaseous diffusion plant, remembered that Young "had a union card in one hand and an NAACP card in the other. African Americans wouldn't be where they are today without the unions."

Dr. Martin Luther King Jr. observed that the labor-hater and the race-baiter were often one and the same. In his 1967 book *Where Do We Go from Here: Chaos or Community?*, Dr. King wrote that

> *the labor movement, especially in its earlier days, was one of the few great institutions where a degree of hospitality and mobility was available to Negroes. While the rest of the nation accepted rank discrimination and prejudice as ordinary and usual...trade unions, particularly in the CIO, leveled all barriers to equal membership. In a number of instances Negroes rose to influential national office.*

W.C. Young was among them.

Young's last office was in the old West Kentucky Building and Construction Trades Council, AFL-CIO, building about one hundred yards from his front doorstep. But for many years, he commuted by car or airliner between an office in Chicago and his Paducah home.

Young traveled many miles for the union movement. He visited all fifty states. In 1993, he journeyed to South Africa representing the AFL-CIO on a mission to find out what Americans could do to help blacks long suffering under apartheid. The trip was made a year before South Africa's first free and open presidential election.

Young was also a veteran civil rights leader. He was a life member of the local NAACP branch. In 1961, he was named to a national panel that advised President John F. Kennedy on civil rights legislation. Three years later, he became an aide to Governor Edward T. Breathitt. During Breathitt's term, Kentucky became the first southern state to pass civil rights legislation.

In 1968, Young became field director of the COPE Minority Department in Washington. He said civil rights leaders "have always known that with the labor movement they have a strong friend with clout."

In 1977, Young was sent to Chicago to be director of COPE Region One, which encompassed seven Midwestern states. After a reorganization, he became head of Region 10, which included Kentucky, Ohio and Tennessee.

Young also loved politics. A devoted Democrat, he helped in many state, local and national campaigns. At age seventy-five, he worked for then congressman Tom Barlow as a field representative.

Young's work on behalf of his church, organized labor, civil rights and his hometown did not go unrecognized. He received many honors, including a 1989 award from the Louisville chapter of the A. Phillip Randolph Institute, a national organization that helps encourage minorities to vote and get involved in the political process. Like Young, Randolph was a national labor and civil rights leader. Young served on the national board of the A. Philip Randolph Institute.

Local labor honored him, too. The highest honor the Paducah-based Western Kentucky Area Council, AFL-CIO, bestows is the W.C. Young Award. Young received the first award in 1994.

In addition, Young was inducted into the Kentucky Civil Rights Hall of Fame in 2003.

Listed in *Who's Who in American Labor*, Young was a keen student of labor history, some of which he made himself.

He believed that labor history should be especially stressed to young trade unionists, whom he once compared to the biblical Israelites Moses led to the Promised Land. "Moses told the children they would have houses they did not build, wells they did not dig and vineyards they did not plant," Young said. "In the trade union movement, we have reached the Promised Land, but some of our young people don't know how hard it was to get there."

Bill Sanders: "Mr. Western Kentucky Labor"

The West Kentucky Building and Construction Trades Council, AFL-CIO, was organized in 1908, the same year W.B. "Bill" Sanders was born.

When Sanders died at age ninety-one, he was still the Paducah union group's executive secretary and possibly the oldest union officer in America.

The Famous and Not So Famous

At ninety, he was at least the "oldest living Building Trades official in the country," according to Robert A. Georgine, president of the AFL-CIO's Building and Construction Trades Department in Washington.

Sanders became council executive secretary when he was seventy-two. Before that, he was president for many years.

Until shortly before he died, Sanders put in forty-hour weeks at his little office in downtown Paducah. He answered the phone with a booming "Building Trades!"

Bill Sanders. *Courtesy of the W.B. Sanders Retirement Center.*

A stocky, barrel-chested native of Corinth, Mississippi, Sanders was born on March 30, 1908. Ten days before and many miles away in Paducah, workers started the West Kentucky Building and Construction Trades Council.

Sanders moved to Paducah and became a trade unionist and a builder at age twenty-five. "Labor is my life," he said about a year before he died. "I wouldn't last a month away from this."

Sanders carried a union card as an ironworker and a carpenter. He was business agent of Ironworkers Local 782 and Carpenters Local 559. He also was executive secretary of the Four Rivers District Council of Carpenters and vice-president of the Kentucky State Building and Construction Trades Council. His Paducah union buddies called him "Mr. Western Kentucky Labor."

His buddies included Larry Sanderson, Gary Seay and Bill Hack. "If I had to describe Bill Sanders in just one word, it would be 'irreplaceable,'" said Sanderson, an international representative for the United Association of Journeymen and Apprentices of the Plumbing and Pipefitting Industry of the United States and Canada. "If he had bled, he would have bled union," said Seay, longtime business manager of International Brotherhood of Electrical Workers Local 816. "He was my mentor—he meant everything to me," said Hack, retired business agent of Local 782.

Sanders joined the Ironworkers in 1933, that grim Depression year when Democrat Franklin D. Roosevelt moved into the White House. "FDR was the greatest president labor ever had," said Sanders, a lifelong Democrat. "There's no doubt about that."

When the United States entered World War II in 1941, Sanders helped recruit volunteers for the Seabees, the navy's storied construction battalions. He signed up so many men that the navy gave him an Award of Merit.

After World War II, Sanders joined the Carpenters and became a leader in the Paducah local. He also became synonymous with the Building Trades Council.

In 1995, Sanders became the second recipient of the W.C. Young Award. Plaques and certificates all over Sanders's office testified to many of the union man's achievements. One of his first honors came in 1933, when he helped build some big gasoline storage tanks in Paducah. The Ironworkers cited him for driving 515 cold rivets in two hours and fifteen minutes, a local record.

If asked which award made him proudest, Sanders would not point to anything hanging on the wall. "It's those two buildings," he would reply. "They were the greatest things organized labor ever did for this community."

Sanders meant two big senior citizens' apartment buildings: the six-story W.B. Sanders Retirement Center and the twenty-story Jackson House, the latter said to be the tallest building in Kentucky west of Louisville. Both were union-constructed under the guidance of Sanders, who also loaned $45,000 of his own savings to help buy land around the Jackson House, which opened in 1974.

"The labor movement is part of the community," Sanders said. "We believe in community—good churches, good government, good jobs, good wages, health and welfare."

Until he died, Sanders was the only president of the Jackson House board of directors. Elected in 1971, he was reelected every two years afterward.

Sanders got the same pay as Jackson House board president that he had received as building trades secretary. "Nothing," he said with a chuckle. "I do this because I love it."

It was that kind of selflessness that made Georgine a Sanders fan. "We are proud of his many years of devoted service and his accomplishments as a leader of the West Kentucky Building Trades Council," Georgine said in honor of Sanders's ninetieth birthday. Later, Georgine wrote Sanders, "I am moved—and humbled—by the sense of mission that has clearly guided you and benefited so many through all those twisted roads we call years."

In addition, the Kentucky General Assembly saluted Sanders with a special resolution when he turned ninety. In part, it read:

The Famous and Not So Famous

His tenacious courage and conviction for the advancement of the labor movement in Kentucky has served as a source of strength and encouragement for others; he is revered by his peers and has unflinchingly given of himself for the rights and needs of working people, and he continues to serve his fellow workers and the entire labor movement with dedication and distinction.

Nobody is likely to top "Mr. Western Kentucky Labor's" sixty-six-year tenure in the union movement, Sanders's union brothers and sisters say.

"You want to know how I get to work every day?" Sanders said after turning ninety. He added with a grin, "With my walking cane and my car. I used to smoke a pipe and ten of those black cigars a day. But I quit that on March 4, 1970. I quit drinking, too, except at Christmas I might have a little glass of wine or something."

Sanders died on July 2, 1999. He was buried in Provine Cemetery in Briensburg in Marshall County. "Bill Sanders was the grandfather of labor in western Kentucky," said Glenn Dowdy, former Area Council president. "We all benefited from his knowledge, wisdom and experience."

Sanders said that more than union members benefit from unions. He remembered a Detroit woman who, almost penniless and down on her luck, got drunk in Paducah and ended up in jail. She had hurt her knee and needed medical attention.

My office is near the jail. The jailer came over to me and told me about her. He said, "Bill, you've got a union meeting this morning. Will you see what you can do?" I said I would, and I asked him how much money she would need. The jailer said, "$500 for her hospital bill and she'll have to have some traveling money, too." Well, we made up all that money. So I went down to the hospital and gave this money to that lady, and she said, "Mr. Sanders, when I get better, I'm going back to Detroit and go back to my husband and try to and work things out." When she got well, she went back to Detroit, joined the church and got back with her husband. That's the kind of things unions do that never get in the paper.

2
OUTRIGHT VILLAINS AND OTHER SHADY CHARACTERS

DID BIG HARP LOSE HIS HEAD TO A WEBSTER WITCH?

Big Harp's head disappeared from Webster County long ago. But J. Harold Utley doubted that a witch stole it.

"I suspect the head weathered away on its own," said Utley, who was a western Kentucky historian. "The Good Book says, 'Dust thou art and to dust thou shall return.'"

Lawmen slew the notorious outlaw Micajah "Big" Harp (sometimes spelled "Harpe") in 1799. They cut off his head and impaled it on a tree limb to scare other criminals.

The gruesome spot is on U.S. Highway 41A north of Dixon, the Webster County seat. "Frontier Justice," explains a Kentucky Historical Society marker at the site.

"It was a crossroads back then, but there's no trace of the crossroads or the tree," said Utley, who lives in Madisonville, the seat of adjacent Hopkins County, which was Harp country, too.

The bloody misdeeds of Big Harp and his equally evil brother, Wiley "Little" Harp, stain the pages of early Kentucky history. Between them, the siblings supposedly killed close to forty people, maybe more, in cold blood. Allegedly, Big Harp's multiple murder victims included his baby son.

Highway marker at Harp's Head.

There are enough Harp tales to last a hundred Halloweens. But no story is eerier than the one about a purported Webster County witch who supposedly swiped Harp's noggin to make a potion.

According to *Spawn of Evil*, a book by Paul I. Wellman, the woman's nephew suffered fits. A "conjuring doctor" told her that human skull bone, "'pulverized and properly concocted,' would cure the malady," Wellman wrote.

One night, the witch sneaked up to the tree, snatched the skull, took it home and pounded it into powder.

"There is no record as to the success or failure of this 'cure' in the case of the nephew with fits," Wellman wrote. There is no record of a head-napping witch either, according to Utley, who was president of the Hopkins County Historical Society and author of articles about the Harps.

The neighborhood where the posse posted Big Harp's head became known as "Harp's Head." The future U.S. 41A was known locally as "Harp's Head Road."

The tree that held Harp's head was still standing in 1874, when Lewis and Richard Collins's *History of Kentucky* was published. "The letters H.H., for

Outright Villains and Other Shady Characters

Harp's Head, carved upon the oak tree at that time (1799), are still legible; and that oak was, from 1811 to 1860, the corner tree of the three counties, Union, Henderson and Hopkins," the history book said.

In 1860, the legislature created Webster County from parts of Henderson, Hopkins and Union Counties. "'Harpe's Head' became so noted a place that even the line of Union County, when formed [in 1811], was made to run past it 'in a direct and straight line,'" Lewis and Richard Collins also wrote.

The Harps were perhaps most notorious as river pirates. Based at the much-feared Cave-In-Rock on the Illinois side of the Ohio River, the brothers ambushed flatboats, robbing and murdering unsuspecting wayfarers.

Afterward, the killers holed up in Webster County with three female companions and their two children. Posing as Methodist ministers for a while, Big and Little Harp slew at least six people.

In one of their most brutal crimes, the Harps murdered a woman and her infant son at night and then burned their cabin. They hoped the firelight would attract Silas McBee, a local lawman whom the Harps planned to kill in an ambush.

Instead, McBee led a six-man posse in hot pursuit of the Harps and their "family," who escaped across Hopkins County into Muhlenberg County. When the posse closed in, Little Harp ran away.

Big Harp, after abandoning the women and children to the tender mercies of the posse, galloped off on horseback. One lawman shot and wounded him; another finished him off.

According to Wellman, the posse member either shot Harp in the body because he didn't want to spoil the head as a trophy or used Harp's own knife to slice off the villain's head while Harp still lived. Reputedly, Harp cursed the man—taunting him to "cut on and be damned!"—and then died.

Harp's executioner was Moses Stegall, whose wife and baby Harp had killed. In yet another strange twist to the story, it has been claimed that Stegall was secretly a Harp confederate who really slew the outlaw to silence him.

In any event, Harp's Head is near where the Harps murdered the Stegalls. "Big Harp's head displayed here as a warning to outlaws," the historical marker says.

"That Skull in Its Ball of Blue Clay"

Samuel Mason was a classic case of a good man gone bad. A Virginia-born Revolutionary War officer, Mason moved west and turned to a life of

The Cave-In-Rock.

crime. In the 1790s, he bossed a band of river pirates around Henderson and Diamond Island, Kentucky, and at Cave-In-Rock.

Mason arrived in Henderson, then called Red Banks, in 1794, according to *It Happened in Southern Illinois* by John Allen. His crime career had begun fourteen years before in Wheeling, Virginia—now West Virginia—where he ran a tavern and was accused of stealing horses. Afterward, he drifted to east Tennessee, where he was accused of cattle rustling and robbing slave cabins. General John Sevier, the famous Tennessee pioneer, ordered Mason to leave, Allen added.

Mason might have become a murderer at Red Banks, where he was counted as one of the community's first settlers. "His daughter, after a clandestine and unconventional courtship, married an infamous character named Kuykendall, much against Mason's wishes," Allen explained.

Mason pretended reconciliation, throwing a big dinner party for the newlyweds. The groom was killed at the soirée, "some thought at Mason's instigation," Allen wrote.

The author added, "At Henderson he began to gather the nucleus of his band." Eventually, local Regulators ran Mason's gang out of town. They retreated to Diamond Island, seventeen miles downriver from Henderson, according to Allen.

After a brief stay on the little island, Mason moved down the Ohio to Cave-In-Rock. "Here, assuming the name of Wilson, the first of several aliases, he arranged living quarters in the cave and placed a sign on the riverbank saying 'Wilson's Liquor Vault and House of [or "for" in other sources] Entertainment.'"

"His hospitality was not of the best," wrote W.D. Snively and Louanna Furbee in *Satan's Ferryman: A True Tale of the Old Frontier*. "The 'liquor vault' portion of the sign spoke for itself. The 'house for entertainment' referred of course to the bordello. Many who tasted Mason's hospitality at the cave did not leave alive."

Mason evidently inspired a movie character. Walter Brennan played Colonel Jeb Hawkins in the 1962 film *How the West Was Won*. Some scenes were shot at Cave-In-Rock.

In the movie, the honest, unsuspecting Linus Rawlings, played by Jimmy Stewart, paddles his canoe up to the cave. Hawkins welcomes him. Jeb's comely daughter, Dora, invites Rawlings deep in the cave to see "the varmint." She stabs him, apparently fatally, but he survives and escapes.

That's Hollywood, not history. Few, if any, of Mason's victims got away alive.

Allen wrote that besides piracy, Mason's gang engaged in horse thievery, slave stealing, kidnapping and "almost any type of crime that offered a profit." The Mason gang's misdeeds multiplied as flatboat traffic increased on the Ohio in the early 1800s. "For the bandits, the unwieldy flatboat was a gift from the gods," Snively and Furbee added. "If they were unable to lure it to the cave or one of their other lairs located on islands up- or downriver, they could always attack it in canoes."

Similarly, Allen wrote that Mason "pursued robbery methodically. Pilots were sent up-river as far as Shawneetown [Illinois] to safely guide boats, as was stated, 'past the dangerous places.'"

Along the way, Mason would post men, who would come out in small craft and invite flatboats to land. Others waited onshore and beckoned the flatboat crews to put in where they were, Allen wrote. "Sometimes armed bands sallied out from the cave rendezvous to forcibly seize boats that ignored invitations. Many boats were robbed, and robbery almost invariably meant murder, for Mason wanted no talkers left. Boats and boatmen continued to vanish along the Cave-In-Rock stretch of the river until the steamboat came."

Mason permitted some boats to pass unmolested, Allen wrote. "Concerning these, Mason is quoted as saying, 'They are taking that load down the river for me,' for returning boatmen were methodically robbed."

Eventually, Mason and his gang moved to the Mississippi River, using remote Wolf Island, near Columbus, as their new pirate den.

Later, Mason shifted his operations inland, turning his pirates into highwaymen on the famous Natchez Trace. In 1803, Mason's sins found him out; he, John Setton and another of his henchmen were captured and brought to trial before a Spanish court at New Madrid, Missouri.

"He appeared there as a cringing, whining prisoner, trying to blame others for all the crimes charged to him," Allen wrote. Since Mason's alleged crimes happened on American soil, Mason, to his surprise, was turned over to American authorities at Natchez, capital of the Mississippi territory. On the way down the Mississippi, Mason and his thugs overpowered their guards and escaped.

The governor of the Mississippi Territory offered a $2,000 reward for Mason, dead or alive, wrote Jonathan Daniels in *The Devil's Backbone: The Story of the Natchez Trace*. Two of Mason's men—James Mays and Setton—proved there is no honor among thieves. They killed him for the reward—Allen said it was $1,000—in late 1803.

The duo claimed they caught the sixty-four-year-old bandit asleep in a swamp near Natchez. Mays and Setton said they tomahawked him to death, according to Daniels.

Mays and Setton knew that to collect the reward they would need proof that they had ended Mason's life. Evidently, they decided his body was too heavy to carry. So they severed the head and rolled it in a ball of blue clay to forestall decay, Daniels wrote.

They lugged their grisly trophy to old Greenville, near Natchez, where the circuit court was in session. Yet Mayes and Sutton received an unexpected and unwanted reward.

While authorities were examining the head, two of Mays and Setton's victims happened by and fingered them as outlaws. Both were arrested, tried, convicted and hanged in early 1804. Their heads were stuck on poles—Setton's north of Natchez, Mays's south of town, according to Daniels.

As it turned out, "Setton" was an alias for a homicidal villain whose equally evil brother's head had suffered the same fate in Kentucky.

John Setton was Little Harpe.

"If the head [Mays and Setton]…was not Mason's, nobody ever heard of Mason again," Daniels wrote. "It is not in the record what happened to that skull in its ball of blue clay."

"The Chief Villain in the Western Country During the Years Between the Revolution and the Civil War"

Many people looked up to Sheriff Jim Ford, a Crittenden County pioneer. They trusted him as their brave protector in a western Kentucky wilderness menaced by murderers, thieves and Ohio River pirates. But nobody ever built a monument to him.

"Everybody who knows the story of Jim Ford knows why," said Chris Evans, publisher of the *Crittenden Press* newspaper in Marion, the county seat. "He also led a gang of robbers and killers. They did the dirty work and kept the bloodstains off his hands."

Eventually, Ford's sins found him out. Vigilantes killed Big Jim, but that's getting ahead of the story.

In the 1820s and 1830s, Sheriff Ford owned a large farm and ran an Ohio River ferry about twelve miles from Marion and two miles or so from Kirksville, now Tolu. All the while, his cutthroats robbed and murdered dozens of unsuspecting migrants on the remote Kentucky and Illinois roads his ferry linked.

Snively and Furbee chronicled Ford's many misdeeds in *Satan's Ferryman*. They said Ford "was the chief villain in the Western country during the years between the Revolution and the Civil War."

Ford's Ferry Road.

The authors added, "Even for a period rife with lawbreakers, his double life was unique. He succeeded in cloaking his outlaw career with a reputation as a leading citizen of his community until it seemed that he was two persons, a veritable Dr. Jekyll and Mr. Hyde."

Ford was named a justice of the peace in 1803, hence his title "Squire Ford." In 1825, Governor Joseph Desha named him sheriff of Livingston County. (Crittenden County was not carved from Livingston County until 1842.) Law-abiding citizens trustingly reported crimes to Sheriff Ford. He would secretly tell lawbreakers to leave for their own good. Ford—and Ford alone—was crime boss of the county. "Word would circulate—no doubt with the help from the Ford's Ferry Gang—that 'Jim Ford found the robbers and ran them out of the country,'" Snively and Furbee wrote.

His robbers hid the bodies of their victims by sinking them in the river or dropping them into a local cavern dubbed "the murder cave." "This whole area was pretty notorious," Evans said. "Ford's Ferry is near Cave-In-Rock. There's an old tombstone in Crittenden County that has 'murdered by the Harpes' chiseled on it."

Outright Villains and Other Shady Characters

Not until July 5, 1833, did frontier justice finally catch up to Jim Ford. Vincent Simpson's murder was the last straw.

James Shouse, one of Ford's thugs, killed Simpson. Armed vigilantes, who called themselves "Regulators," figured out that Ford was behind the slaying.

The Regulators took Ford to his log cabin office next to the ferry landing. They would make him forfeit his life near where his henchmen had shed so much innocent blood.

The Regulators offered the condemned man a last meal. The sheriff declined; he guessed he soon would be supping in hell, Snively and Furbee wrote.

The authors wrote that the Regulators sat Big Jim in a chair on the porch of the ferry office. The muzzle of a shotgun was stuck through the logs a few inches from Ford's back.

Inside, with his finger on the trigger, was Simpson's young son. When the Regulators gave the word, the lad fired. "There was a muffled roar, then a crash as Ford's heavy body fell," Snively and Furbee wrote.

The Regulators later insisted that somebody shot Big Jim from the dark while they were eating supper inside the ferry office, according to Snively and Furbee.

In any event, it took two days to build an oversize coffin for Ford. He was better than six feet tall and weighed three hundred pounds, the authors wrote.

Nightfall and a thunderstorm were approaching on July 7 when an ox-drawn wagon bore Jim Ford to his final resting place, the Ford family cemetery close to Tolu. (The gravestones, including Ford's, are broken and lying flat in weeds and underbrush in a thicket of trees.)

The funeral cortege consisted of a family friend and some slaves. They hoisted the coffin from the wagon and placed it on two wooden rails laid across the grave. Suddenly, the rail supporting the head of the coffin broke, dumping Ford's remains headfirst into the pit, Snively and Furbee wrote.

Ford's friend pulled his pistol and ordered the slaves into the hole to straighten the coffin. Just then, a loud thunderclap heralded the storm's arrival. With rain coming down in sheets, the slaves climbed out and hastily buried Jim Ford head down.

Local legend has it that an elderly Kirksville slave, whom other slaves believed was a seer, said he had a vision the very instant "the thunderclap sounded," Snively and Furbee wrote. "He told all who would listen that he had seen Squire Ford plunge headfirst into hell."

"He Expressed Considerable Emotion of Joy that He Had Failed in His Efforts of Self-Destruction"

Logan County is a fertile field for Jesse James stories. The James gang held up the Southern Bank of Kentucky in Russellville, the county seat, in 1868. The heist was said to be the gang's first bank robbery. Yet Jesse himself might not have been one of the gun-toting desperados.

"But our Jesse James story is true, for sure," said Becky Tinch, retired city clerk in Adairville, in deep southern Logan County. "Jesse James tried to commit suicide near Adairville."

Tinch has a file to prove it. "It happened at a two-story house west of Adairville that's still standing," she said. "It's on J.C. Holman Road."

The home, long since abandoned, belonged to Jesse and Frank James's aunt and uncle, Nancy and George Hite. The brothers often hid from the law in the dwelling built before the Civil War.

Jesse attempted to take his own life—then thought better of it—in 1869 or 1870.

When he and Frank arrived at the Hites', their sister, Susan James, was already there. She and Jesse quarreled over her plans to marry an ex-Confederate guerrilla who had ridden with Jesse in the Civil War.

The argument added to Jesse's distress. A chest wound from the war had reopened, causing him considerable discomfort.

He had been using morphine as a painkiller and decided to take a lethal overdose. But after swallowing sixteen grains of the powerful narcotic, Jesse decided life was worth living after all.

Tinch has a copy of a *Kansas City Journal* letter-to-the-editor

Jesse James. *Courtesy of the Library of Congress.*

Outright Villains and Other Shady Characters

written by the Adairville physician summoned to save the outlaw. Dr. D.G. Simmons kept quiet until after Bob Ford shot and killed Jesse in 1882. A member of the James gang, Ford gunned down Jesse in St. Joseph, Missouri.

Frank was the outlaw's real savior, according to Simmons. The doctor confessed that his "appeals and circumambulatory stimulants" failed.

In desperation, he turned to Frank, asking if "there was anything or any subject that would, more than anything else, be likely to excite him." Simmons hoped that Jesse might be kept awake until the drug's deadly effect wore off.

Frank whispered in Jesse's ear "certain warning words...as if certain persons who were very obnoxious to him were coming and it was very necessary to escape or defend to the death." The doctor explained that "whenever he seemed to sink into the fatal narcotism, Frank's cabalistics" would bring Jesse to his feet.

While Frank and Susan walked the staggering Jesse around the room, he would brandish his pistols at imaginary enemies. When Jesse relapsed "into profound slumber, even while walking," he was "instantly aroused again by the same talisman," Simmons wrote.

The old Hite house.

At 4:00 a.m., it looked like Jesse was a goner. "His pulse had reduced in volume to a mere thread, his breathing was feeble and very slow and it seemed the death angel was hovering home, ready in a few minutes to seize his prey," the doctor wrote.

Simmons suggested that Jesse be allowed to rest. Perhaps a respite would save him.

"I sat with my finger on the pulse for perhaps an hour, when it began to show evidence of improvement with greater regularity and with more frequent and natural breathing," the doctor wrote.

Jesse seemed on the mend.

By 6:00 a.m., the outlaw had recovered enough to recognize Frank, Susie and his aunt and uncle. Soon afterward, Jesse announced he was ready for breakfast.

"When consciousness was thoroughly aroused he expressed considerable emotion of joy that he had failed in his efforts of self destruction, and was profuse in his thanks to Mrs. Hite and to all parties for their strenuous efforts throughout the night to restore him," Simmons wrote. "He evinced both shame and contrition for his act."

Susan was wed in 1870. "Jesse may have been concerned about the marriage, but most writers prefer to believe that the overdose of morphine was motivated by his pain and not despair over his sister's decision," wrote Philip W. Steele in *Jesse and Frank James: The Family History*. "Jesse was later embarrassed over the incident."

JESSE JAMES, THE JUDGE AND THE TWICE-SWIPED WATCH

Did Jesse James die keeping time with a watch he stole in a stagecoach robbery near Mammoth Cave?

When the famous outlaw was gunned down, Rutherford Harrison Rowntree's $150 gold pocket watch was purportedly found on his person.

Rowntree, sixty-seven, was robbed on September 3, 1880, in a headline-grabbing heist between Mammoth Cave and Cave City. Two masked gunmen escaped with "several hundred dollars worth of watches and jewelry and nearly a thousand dollars in cash," C. Walker Goller wrote in the *Filson Club History Quarterly*.

Authorities discovered Rowntree's watch in Jesse's pocket after Ford slew the outlaw chieftain.

Outright Villains and Other Shady Characters

Soon afterward, another of James's partners in crime admitted that he and James had held up the Mammoth Cave stage. His confession led to the release of an ex-schoolteacher who was facing prison for the robbery, Goller wrote.

Nobody got hurt in the holdup close to the site of Little Hope Baptist Church, near the site of Mammoth Cave National Park. The cave was a tourist attraction even in the 1880s. Stagecoaches shuttled sightseers between the Cave City railroad depot and the celebrated cavern, Goller wrote. The old road became Kentucky Highways 70 and 255.

Rowntree was a well-heeled lawyer and bank president from Lebanon, the Marion County seat. A former county clerk, he was called "Judge Rowntree" out of respect, Goller wrote.

Rowntree, his daughter and nephew, four other passengers and the driver were aboard the stage when the bandit duo struck. Pulling pistols, they ordered the driver to stop the stage "in a thicket just past the Little Hope Baptist Church," according to Goller.

Apparently feeling generous, the highwaymen invited their victims to take a swig from a bottle of whiskey they had swiped from a passenger. They also returned the tourists' railroad tickets before galloping away with their ill-gotten gains, Goller wrote.

Lawmen searched in vain for the thieves. Finally, in November, Thomas J. Hunt of Ohio County was arrested in connection with the robbery. A coal miner, he had taught school in the Cave City neighborhood but recently "had left the area under controversial circumstances," Goller explained.

Jailed in Glasgow, Hunt protested his innocence. Nonetheless, he was indicted for robbery in 1881 and convicted a year later. The jury recommended a three-year sentence.

Hunt was languishing in the Glasgow lockup awaiting formal sentencing when Ford slew James. With the desperado's demise, Bill "Whiskey Head" Ryan, a James sidekick imprisoned for train robbery in Missouri, admitted that he and James had stuck up the Mammoth Cave stage.

"Lenient Luke" Blackburn, Kentucky's governor, pardoned Hunt, who "fled back to his family in Ohio County," Goller wrote. Rowntree was reunited with his watch, which became a family heirloom.

In 1964, Rowntree's descendants donated the well-traveled timepiece to the Louisville-based Filson Historical Society. Three years later, the watch disappeared in a burglary and was never recovered, according to Goller, who suggested that the unknown thief was "a modern-day Jesse James."

"The Great Diamond Fraud"

The *San Francisco Chronicle* called the scam "the most gigantic and barefaced swindle of the ages." The alleged con men were cousins Philip Arnold and John Slack of Elizabethtown, the Hardin County seat.

Purported perpetrators of the "Great Diamond Fraud," the duo is said to have pocketed $660,000. The scheme was discovered, but neither Kentuckian did time for the crime.

Arnold and Slack supposedly pulled off their con in 1871. Posing as poor prospectors, they deposited a sack of uncut diamonds in a San Francisco bank, according to the late Mary Josephine Jones, an Elizabethtown historian and author of *Diamonds, Rubies and Sand: The Story of Philip Arnold of the Great Diamond Fraud and His Connection with Elizabethtown, Kentucky.*

"Arnold and Slack claimed they found the diamonds in a desert sort of place in northwestern Colorado," said Jones, who based her book on research by her late mother, Margaret Settle Richerson.

William C. Ralston, a wealthy San Francisco banker, took Arnold and Slack for rubes. He aimed to cheat them out of the mine, which he figured must be worth millions of dollars.

The gems were genuine, but not the mine. "Arnold and Slack had salted the place with industrial diamonds, rubies, emeralds and sapphires," Jones said.

At first, the trick fooled experts who examined the precious stones or inspected the mine site.

Ralston organized a mining company with $10 million in capital, Jones said. He paid Arnold and Slack $660,000, she added.

In 1872, a geologist and government surveyor visited the site. He pronounced it bogus and thus exposed the fraud.

Arnold and Slack apparently got the industrial diamonds in Europe and from a California drilling company where Arnold worked. They evidently bought the rubies, emeralds and sapphires from Indians who lived elsewhere.

Arnold went home to Elizabethtown with his family. He bought a big house and a bank, apparently with his ill-gotten gains.

A California investor sued Slack and Arnold, seeking to recover $350,000. Arnold paid the plaintiff $150,000 or $250,000—the exact sum is evidently unknown—in an out-of-court settlement, according to Jones.

Though an apparently popular local businessman, Arnold made an enemy of rival banker Harry Holdsworth. The two shot it out in a local saloon in 1878.

Arnold fired his pistol at Holdsworth but missed. Holdsworth, armed with a shotgun, winged Arnold in the shoulder. Two bystanders were wounded.

Arnold survived his wound only to die of pneumonia in 1879. He was forty-nine.

"His funeral was said to have been the largest ever in Elizabethtown," Jones said. "His grave marker was said to be the tallest in Elizabethtown Cemetery."

Slack apparently never married. He became an undertaker and cabinetmaker in White Oaks, New Mexico, where he died at age seventy-six in 1896.

Arnold's partner was a big spender, or he received only a fraction of the $660,000. "The entire value of his estate was $1,611.14," Jones wrote in her book. She quoted a White Oaks paper that said Slack was "one of the oldest and most universally respected citizens of White Oaks."

"You Will Make Any Woman's Boy a Disgrace You Ought to Be Ashamed"

Before she arrived in Elizabethtown, "one of those bad rum-towns in Kentucky," Carry Nation claimed she had never had to spill her blood fighting the Demon Rum. But when the hatchet-wielding, Kentucky-born, anti-alcohol crusader insulted Elizabethtown saloonkeeper J.R. Neighbors in 1904, he bashed her with a chair. The scene is reenacted every summer as part of a local outdoor theater program that features famous folk with Elizabethtown ties.

Local foes of alcohol hated Neighbors even before Nation hit town. She made him an arch-villain in her autobiography, *The Use and Need of the Life of Carry A. Nation*.

The reenactment of the Neighbors-Nation confrontation looks real, said Kenny Tabb, Hardin County clerk. He added that a Good Samaritan once tried to rescue the fallen Nation. It was not in the script, either. Tabb explained:

> *The woman who played Carry came around the corner with fake blood on her head. She was moaning and groaning and saying that J.R. Neighbors just hit her. He's back behind her chasing her. A man was driving by in his car, ran over and tried to help her. The crowd loved it.*

The real Carry Nation was a Garrard County native who moved to Kansas, where she joined the Woman's Christian Temperance Union. She spent the rest of her life speaking and writing passionately against boozing and bars.

She backed up her tough words with tougher deeds. Nicknamed the "Kansas Cyclone," Nation was best known for wrecking saloons with her trusty hatchet. But Neighbors's Elizabethtown watering hole was not among them.

He launched what may have been a preemptive strike against a Nation "hatchitation." The Cyclone blew into Elizabethtown for a temperance lecture. The date was July 23, 1904, according to her book.

Nation recalled that en route to the hall where she was to speak, she stopped and chided Neighbors:

Carry Nation. *Courtesy of the Library of Congress.*

> *Walking into his saloon, [I] said, why are you in this business, drugging and robbing the people? "Hush! You get out." I replied, "Yes you want a respectable woman to get out, but you will make any woman's boy a disgrace, you ought to be ashamed."*

Nation said she then left for the lecture. When she re-passed the saloon after the lecture, she spotted Neighbors sitting in a chair out front. Nation said she asked him if he was the owner.

He replied with "an oath," rose, "picked up the chair and with all his strength, sent it down with a crash on my head," Nation wrote. "I came near falling, caught myself and he lifted the chair the second time, striking me over the back, the blood began to cover my face, and run down from a cut on my forehead.'"

Nation said she cried, "He has killed me!" She added that a police officer showed up in the nick of time, grabbing "the chair to prevent a third blow."

The commotion drew a crowd. "There were two officers in the crowd," Nation wrote. "I cried out, 'Is there no one to arrest this man?' No one appeared to do it."

Outright Villains and Other Shady Characters

Neighbors went back in his saloon. Bloody but unbowed, Nation went to her hotel. "Some one sent for a doctor who came and dressed the wound on my forehead, my left arm was badly bruised, also my back."

Meanwhile, the town had turned on Neighbors. "The women and men came to see me indignant, saying this outrage would not be tolerated," Nation wrote. "The Methodist minister especially was deeply moved."

The next morning, a Mrs. Betty James, who lived two miles from Elizabethtown, arrived in the county seat with a warrant for Neighbors's arrest. "But the case was laid over to await the action of the 'Grand Jury,' in November," Nation wrote, adding that Neighbors was set free on bond.

Nation had planned to travel to Mammoth Cave but remained in Elizabethtown because of the warrant and agreed to give another speech that night. "Elizabethtown is one of those bad rum-towns in Kentucky, but there is a fine prohibition sentiment, and great indignation was felt and expressed that a saloon-keeper even so low and cowardly as to strike a woman, should be tolerated," she wrote. "I was in bed most of the day and nearly fainted during the lecture, but I thanked God that I was counted worthy to suffer, that others might not."

She explained:

> *I felt some mother might receive fewer blows—that while my head was bruised and bleeding to prevent hearts from being crushed and broken, souls were going to drunkards graves, and drunkards Hells, and this outrage would reveal the enormous brutality of this curse, bringing a speedy remedy.*

In her second speech, Nation said Neighbors's assault on her "was the first time she had had to shed blood for her cause!" Guy Winstead wrote in *Chronicles of Hardin County, Kentucky, 1766–1974*.

The Grand Jury indicted Neighbors for assault and battery. He was tried and found guilty in March 1905 and fined fifteen dollars.

3
Tragedies

Hopkinsville Park Commemorates Trail of Tears Deaths

Chief Whitepath and the Cherokees helped General Andrew Jackson beat the Creek Indians in the famous Battle of Horseshoe Bend, Alabama.

"We don't know if Whitepath was sorry about that later," said Midge Durbin, a Hopkinsville history enthusiast. When Jackson became president, he made the Cherokees and other eastern tribes move to Oklahoma.

Buried in Hopkinsville, Whitepath was one of four thousand Cherokees who perished on the notorious Trail of Tears in 1838–39. He was seventy-seven.

The graves of Whitepath; Fly Smith, another tribal leader; and two unknown Cherokees are preserved at the Trail of Tears Park. "We still have the original four limestone markers," said Durbin, a park volunteer. "We also have headstones and life-size bronze statues of Whitepath and Smith."

Backed by Jackson and approved by Congress, the Indian Removal Act of 1830 forced tribes living east of the Mississippi River to migrate to western lands. Old Hickory's successor, President Martin Van Buren, finished the "Indian removal." "The cost in human life cannot be accurately measured, in suffering not even roughly measured," historian Howard Zinn wrote in his book *A People's History of the United States*. "Most of the history books given to children pass quickly over it."

Trail of Tears memorial, Hopkinsville.

The Cherokees were the last Native Americans to go to Oklahoma, then the Indian Territory. They named their grueling eight-hundred-mile trek the Trail of Tears.

Hopkinsville was a Kentucky stop for the Cherokees, who left their homelands in Tennessee, Alabama, North Carolina and Georgia. Guarded by soldiers, more than sixteen thousand Cherokees traveled the trail on foot, astride horses or in wagons.

Tragedies

Many were shoeless. Food, shelter, blankets and warm clothing were in short supply. Indians died almost daily; most were buried along the trail where they succumbed, mainly to exposure, exhaustion or illness.

Two dozen years before, Whitepath, who lived in Georgia, and the Cherokees had been Jackson's allies against the Creeks, who were feared warriors. "You've heard the expression, 'I'll be there if the Creek don't rise?' That's where it came from," Durbin said.

Jackson's troops and their Cherokee allies decisively whipped the Creeks at Horseshoe Bend in 1814. Before Old Hickory attacked, Whitepath and Chief John Ross reportedly swam across the Tallapoosa River and stole the Creek canoes, thus preventing the enemy's escape.

Grouped in bands of about twelve hundred, the Cherokees arrived in Hopkinsville in the fall of 1838. The park is at the old Cherokee campsite on Little River, a tiny stream that meanders through the Christian County seat.

"The Indians were a source of great curiosity and interest to the citizens," Charles Mayfield Meacham wrote in his 1930 *History of Christian County from Oxcart to Airplane*. Smith, who had served on the Cherokee council, "was very old, broken in spirit, and travel worn," Meacham wrote. Whitepath, too, was "old and feeble and much exhausted by travel."

The Trail of Tears Park, which includes a 160-year-old restored log cabin filled with Cherokee history exhibits, also hosts an intertribal powwow every September. Many Cherokees attend. Some of their ancestors came through Hopkinsville on the Trail of Tears, Durbin said.

Zinn added:

> *As they moved westward, they began to die—of sickness, of drought, of the heat, of exposure. There were 645 wagons, and people marching alongside. Survivors, years later, told of halting at the edge of the Mississippi in the middle of winter, the river running full of ice, "hundreds of sick and dying penned up in wagons or stretched upon the ground." Grant Foreman, the leading authority on Indian removal, estimates that during confinement in the stockade or on the march westward four thousand Cherokees died.*

"Men Would Shoot Boys, Boys Would Shoot Men"

Nobody knows what caused the bad blood between the Darnells and Watsons in Madrid Bend. The long-ago feud might have started over a horse or a cow. Nobody seems to know for sure.

Mark Twain wrote about the feud, claiming, "In no part of the South has the vendetta flourished more briskly, or held out longer between warring families, than in this particular region." But he did not say what begat the bloodshed in westernmost Kentucky.

Madrid Bend is that tiny, townless, teardrop-shaped section of Fulton County pinched off from the rest of the state by a big loop in the Mississippi River. By road, the only way into the sparsely populated, ten-square-mile bend is from Tennessee.

Peace prevails in Madrid Bend, where giant cottonwood trees tower over soybean fields as flat and green as pool table tops. But here Watsons and Darnells supposedly slew each other for sixty years before the remaining Watsons wiped out the last of their sworn enemies.

The Darnell-Watson vendetta isn't as famous as the Hatfield-McCoy feud of eastern Kentucky and West Virginia. One of the few accounts of the Madrid Bend mayhem is in Twain's *Life on the Mississippi*, published in 1883. Reportedly, the killings were the inspiration for the Grangerford-Shepherdson feud in Twain's famous novel *Huckleberry Finn*.

Life on the Mississippi is partly a Twain travelogue based on a trip he took down the river after he became a successful writer. A fellow passenger, who says he lived near Madrid Bend, tells Twain about the Darnell-Watson feud:

> *Every year or so, somebody was shot, on one side or the other; and as fast as one generation was laid out, their sons took up the feud and kept it a-going. And it's just as I say; they went on shooting each other, year in and year out—making a kind of religion of it, you see—till they'd done forgot, long ago, what it was all about. Whenever a Darnell caught a Watson, or a Watson caught a Darnell, one of 'em was going to get hurt—only question was, which of them got the drop on the other. They'd shoot each other down, right in the presence of the family. They didn't hunt for each other, but when they happened to meet, they pulled and begun. Men would shoot boys, boys would shoot men. A man shot a boy twelve years old—happened on him in the woods, and didn't give him no chance. If he had a' given him a chance, the boy'd a' shot him.*

Tragedies

The passenger also says that the rival families worshipped at a little church that straddled the Kentucky-Tennessee state line. The spot was called Compromise Landing. Supposedly, half the church was in Kentucky and the other half was in Tennessee.

Twain's traveling companion explains:

> *They lived each side of the line…Sundays you'd see the families drive up, all in their Sunday clothes, men, women, and children, and file up the aisle, and set down, quiet and orderly, one lot on the Tennessee side of the church and the other on the Kentucky side; and the men and boys would lean their guns up against the wall, handy, and then all hands would join in with the prayer and praise; though they say the man next the aisle didn't kneel down, along with the rest of the family; kind of stood guard.*

The passenger says surviving Darnells or Watsons didn't know why their forebears took up killing each other. "Some says it was about a horse or a cow—anyway, it was a little matter; the money in it wasn't of no consequence—none in the world—both families was rich."

"One of the Most Desperate Affrays Ever Known in Western Kentucky"

It was Christmas Eve 1900, but Graves County sheriff Sam Douthitt aimed to arrest Burch Hollier anyway.

An accused bootlegger, Hollier was holed up in Mayfield, the county seat, at the house of his father-in-law, Charles Bolin. Douthitt and Deputy John Bunyan Usher, armed with pistols and riding horses, arrived at Bolin's place about 10:00 p.m.

Usher's saddlebags bulged with Christmas toys for his four kids, who probably would be asleep by the time he got home. The deputy might have figured he would have plenty of time to play Santa Claus before Christmas morning.

John Bunyan Usher didn't come home. "Bolin killed him and the sheriff killed Bolin," said Ray Usher, the deputy's grandson.

The murder of Deputy Usher, thirty-three, is all but forgotten in Mayfield. Even so, the *Paducah News* pronounced the gunfight "one of the most desperate affrays ever known in Western Kentucky…Mayfield has had many big sensations, but this double killing is perhaps the greatest in her history," the paper added.

Deputy Usher, his wife and one of their children. *Courtesy of Dale Usher.*

Tragedies

Ray Usher didn't know his grandfather. "My father, Wilber Usher, was 2½ when his father was killed," he said.

The Usher family treasures a pair of dolls from their ancestor's saddlebags. "One was for my father and the other one for my Aunt Ethel," Ray Usher said. "One is a china doll, and the other is what they called a chalk doll."

Ray Usher also has a clipping from the December 26, 1900 *Paducah News* that tells about the shootout. Usher reportedly was the fifth man whose life Bolin had snuffed out.

Hollier, whose nickname was "Bull," peddled booze "from Illinois to Mayfield," according to the *News*. Shortly before the shootout, a Graves County Grand Jury had indicted him "for violation of the local option law," the Paducah paper reported.

Usher grave marker near Mayfield.

Hollier's father-in-law was a worse character, according to the *News*. "Bolin was from the notorious Boydsville section down on the Tennessee line. He has often been in trouble and it is said had killed four men prior to coming to Mayfield."

Douthitt evidently expected trouble from Hollier, so he took Usher as backup. Usher was the sheriff's "best deputy," the *News* said.

When Usher told Hollier he was under arrest, the alleged bootlegger pulled a pistol and shot at the deputy but missed him. "Usher was just in the act of leveling his pistol at Hollier, when Bolin drew a big Smith & Wesson pistol and shot him four times," the *News* said. "The brave officer was dead before he could pull the trigger of his weapon."

Bolin drew a bead on Douthitt, but the sheriff swatted Bolin's arm, knocking the handgun upward. The pistol went off so close to Douthitt's face that the muzzle "flash burned his moustache off," the *News* claimed.

Unfazed, the sheriff shot Bolin in the head, killing him instantly. Douthitt also fired at Hollier, grazed his skull and forced him to surrender.

Hollier was jailed in Mayfield, where he risked lynching for "being the cause of the tragedy," the *News* said. The paper also predicted that the "worthless young outlaw" would be legally hanged for trying to kill Douthitt. Hollier's fate is evidently unknown.

Death on the Ohio

There is nothing at Turner's Landing to commemorate the spot where "heroism and cowardice, death and destruction, met in a scene unparalleled in the history of the lower Ohio."

On a terror-filled night in 1902, seventy men, women and children died when the steamer *City of Pittsburgh*, longer than a football field, burned up on the Ohio River near Turner's Landing in Ballard County. It was one of the worst marine disasters in American history, yet the exact spot were the riverboat crashed into the bank has evidently been forgotten.

The loss of the *Pittsburgh* has been compared to the sinking of the *Titanic* ten years later, almost to the day. Lifeboats were in short supply on both doomed vessels. Both tragedies happened at night, and many people drowned in cold, dark water. But while the *Titanic* was lost in the deep Atlantic Ocean, the *Pittsburgh* ran aground, burned and sank in shallow water on April 20, 1902.

Nothing on the remote Ohio River riverbank around Turner's Landing speaks of the disaster that struck while most of the *Pittsburgh*'s 145 passengers and crew were fast asleep. Fire broke out about 4:00 a.m. in a cargo of hay. Supposedly, a carelessly dropped cigarette ignited the blaze aboard the three-year-old boat, which was painted gleaming white with bright red trim.

With the front end of his vessel engulfed in flames, pilot Harry Doss managed to beach it. Nonetheless, the fire quickly spread. The *Paducah News-Democrat* reported "blazes curling into the air a hundred feet," planks "consumed like coal-oil" and "woodwork…crackling a song of death and destruction."

The boat's roof, made of tarpaper, "was licked up like shavings." Its twin smokestacks and big calliope crashed into the inferno, according to the newspaper.

There was no hint of trouble when the *Pittsburgh*, bound from Cincinnati to Cairo, Illinois, called at Paducah. A clerk at the waterfront logged it in at 10:30 p.m. on April 19.

The *Pittsburgh* steamed away about 2:00 a.m., its huge, side-mounted paddle wheels churning the wide, dark river to a froth. Two hours later and thirty miles downstream, "heroism and cowardice, death and destruction, met in a scene unparalleled in the history of the lower Ohio River," the *News-Democrat* said.

The fire killed many passengers and crew in their beds and drove others aft. The flames overtook some, while others jumped overboard, trusting their fates to the cold, black water. Many "struggled and screamed and prayed, and went down to death with their last words gurgling on their lips," the newspaper said.

A number of passengers got away in a little yawl, the only lifeboat available. Fire consumed the oars. But the *City of Pittsburgh* crew paddled the boat with their bare hands, splashing to and from the riverbank, rescuing survivors from the water and the inferno.

Harry Doss swam to safety. Also surviving was pilot Al Pritchard, whose wife and their two children were aboard. He was on the way to relieve Doss when the fire was discovered. Doss told him to go back and save his family.

Apparently, Pritchard was not present when his family got aboard the yawl. Their six-year-old daughter hit her head on the lifeboat and fell into the river. "She held out her arms and screamed to her mother to save her," the *News-Democrat* said. "This the mother was powerless to do and she had to watch her little girl drown a few feet away."

Whole families also perished. Few losses were greater than that of the Burts of Owensboro. Patrick Burt, his wife and ten of their eleven children were killed. Only five-year-old Lily and the family dog escaped.

Many who got away from the flames collapsed, exhausted, in a nearby clearing. Several survivors swam ashore in their nightclothes and were soaking wet. Mosquitoes showed no mercy, swarming them. Several people became ill and were "swollen from head to foot" from repeated stings, according to the *News-Democrat*.

Shortly before noon on April 20, another steamboat transported the survivors fifteen miles downriver to Cairo. "Some left children in the debris, some left husbands, others wives, and nearly all left friends," the *News-Democrat* reported. "The survivors quit the scene with tears flowing from their eyes and prayers for the dead."

"The Daughter of the King of Kings"

Was Paducah's "Orphan Annie" the inspiration for the famous comic strip character? She probably was not. Yet this real Annie's life was short and tragic.

"Orphan Annie's" tombstone, Paducah.

She was a loving, brown-eyed little girl who perished at age ten. Annie never knew her last name or her birthday, according to a 1964 *Paducah Sun-Democrat* newspaper story written on the fiftieth anniversary of the child's death.

Annie was born in eastern Kentucky, though exactly when was evidently unknown. Her family was poor; Annie's parents were gunned down in a blood feud.

A Paducah Presbyterian pastor and his wife adopted her. Annie came to love her father and mother. They loved her too.

Annie said she wanted to be a Presbyterian missionary when she grew up. But the child died after she was injected with vaccine doctors did not know was tainted. She lay bedridden and gravely ill for three months.

Annie succumbed the day after her doctor said that if she could hang on for just twenty-four hours more, she would pull through.

Annie spent her last hours in wonderment at a bright red sky, blooming peach trees and dandelions, which she saw only in her mind's eye. But she heard Easter music.

Tragedies

The last word Annie uttered was "mother," according to Mary A. Burrell, her mother. She and her husband, the Reverend Henry Burrell, pastor of Paducah First Presbyterian Church, were the only family Annie knew.

The *Sun-Democrat* story, written by Bill Powell, who later wrote for the *Louisville Courier-Journal*, contained Mary Burrell's reminiscences of Annie's life.

Mary met Annie at an orphans' home in Balfour, North Carolina. Annie was a troublesome waif who seemed bound for reform school.

Mary, who was spending the summer of 1912 at nearby Montreat, North Carolina, stayed a while at the orphanage. She saw Annie, who was about eight years old, and wanted her, according to Powell.

Never mind that the child apparently stole Mary's rings and also made off with eleven jars of apple jelly and a set of woven table mats. "Notwithstanding all we had gone through, I could not leave Annie at the orphanage without leaving a part of myself, because I had become so interested in her," Powell quoted Mary.

She wrote a letter to her husband proposing that they adopt Annie. He agreed and sent his wife fifteen dollars to cover the train trip from North Carolina to Paducah. Annie snatched the bills and burned them in a stove. But that night, Powell wrote, Annie had a sudden and dramatic change of heart.

"God, I do want to go to 'Pawducah.' God give me fifteen dollars," she prayed.

Mary recalled that Annie maintained a prayer vigil for four nights. The orphan's would-be mother could hardly believe her eyes when she opened a letter from Paducah on the fifth day. A check for fifteen dollars tumbled out of the envelope, according to Powell.

Ada Eaton, head nurse at the Illinois Central Railroad Hospital, had written Mary. Mary explained, "In her letter she said, 'I read an article the other day which said, 'If you love someone, tell them so, write them a letter, or, better still, send them a check. I am doing all three. The check is for a bit of pin money. Love, Ada Eaton.'"

The letter came with a postscript: "I don't know why, but for 30 days this has been on my desk, not mailed."

When Annie reached Paducah, she beamed and said her new hometown was "des like heaven," according to Mary.

Having stopped her stealing, Annie was ready to join the Presbyterian Church, Mary said. "With her perfect complexion and her large brown eyes, she was an entirely different child from the one we had taken."

Annie decided to join the church at the close of an evening service. The congregation was singing the last hymn, "More Like the Master I Would Be."

"I must join the church to that," she whispered to her mother.

Annie slipped from the pew and walked down the aisle to the pulpit. Reverend Burrell announced that Annie wanted to be a member.

He immediately called together the session, or the board of elders. "There was not a dry eye at the meeting of the session," Mary wrote.

She and her husband planned to educate Annie to be a missionary. She was to return to her native Appalachia.

"She would say, 'I'll go missionary them, but you and Mr. Burrell will have to go with me," Mary explained.

Annie never got to "missionary" anywhere. She fell fatally ill in midwinter 1914.

Mary recalled that school authorities asked that Annie be re-vaccinated, evidently against smallpox. The first vaccination had not taken.

Soon afterward, Annie became gravely ill. She was unable to eat. "In all that time she never complained once or said, 'Why did they do this to me?'" Mary wrote.

Articles about Annie appeared in local newspapers. Flowers from well-wishers filled her room at the Burrell home.

Annie battled her illness into spring. Her doctor playfully dubbed her "Tom." The day before the little girl died, he told Mary that if Annie could hold out just a day longer, she would survive.

"If I des had something to give you and Mr. Burrell," she told her mother. "Annie, you have given us your love, and what more could anyone give?" Mary replied. "I'll des turn over here and ask God to give you something for me," Annie responded.

The child rolled over. Her lips moved in silent prayer.

"The next day, Mr. Earl Palmer, who was not a member of any church, wrote a letter to Dr. Burrell and myself, and said, 'I am enclosing a check for $50 for you both, in the name of little Mountain Annie," Mary added.

The day Annie died, she spoke of a beautiful sky outside her window, all lovely and red, even though the shades were drawn.

Fearing Annie's life was ebbing away, Mary summoned the doctor. According to Mary, the first words he spoke after he arrived were, "Did you notice that bright spot in the sky? I have never seen anything like it."

When the physician came into her room, Annie looked into his eyes. She said she loved him and thanked him "for everything."

The doctor turned away. He began to cry. "Tom, I love you, too," he said. "You've made a man out of me. I was not even a Christian when I walked into your room the first time."

He left and returned again at noon.

Earlier, Annie had commented about the peach trees and "dangylions" being in bloom. "Oh, if I des had something to give you and Mr. Burrell," she said again about 1:00 p.m.

Mary wrote that the choir was rehearsing for the Easter service next door at the church. "I'm so glad my room is on this side of the house, so I can hear them practicing the Easter music," Annie said.

Annie looked lovingly at her parents. "I have such a good father," she said to Reverend Burrell. "And such a good mother," she said to Mary.

Her lips stopped moving. Annie was dead.

The child was first buried in Paducah's Oak Grove Cemetery. "Four little girls were pallbearers for Orphan Annie, who never went by a last name after she joined the minister and his wife," Powell wrote.

Virginia Hart was one of the pallbearers. In the 1930s, Annie's remains were transferred to Mount Kenton Cemetery and buried on part of Hart's family plot. At Mary's behest, she had a small footstone placed over the grave. "MARY A. BURRELLS 'ORPHAN ANNIE,'" the epitaph reads.

"Mrs. Burrell's great love for Little Orphan Annie, who lived in the Burrell home only two eventful years, never waned," Powell wrote. "In her old days she asked Mrs. Hart to put up the monument and to see that nothing ever happened to the stone."

The little gray slab is still there.

Meanwhile, hundreds of people had flocked to Annie's funeral service. Many viewed her grave, which was blanketed with flowers.

The day after the service, the Burrells were back at Oak Grove. A man walked up to them. He said he wanted to see the grave of a child he was told must have been a millionaire's daughter.

"No, just a poor little orphan girl from the mountains," came the reply, according to Powell's story, "but the daughter of the King of Kings."

"A SAILOR BOY DONE IT"

Their old gray tombstone in Mayfield's Maplewood Cemetery tells a tragic tale.

"In memory of the LAWRENCE & DREW Families," the epitaph reads. "Eleven in number who met a horrible Death in the burning of the Lawrence home near Hickory, Ky., on the night of June 25, 1921—One of the unsolved Mysteries."

Lawrence and Drew family tombstone, Mayfield.

Buried beneath the tombstone is a single coffin that holds the charred remains of four adults and seven children. All perished in the blaze that destroyed Ernest Lawrence's little log cabin about three miles from Hickory in north Graves County.

"Murder, insanity, arson or destiny, one, two, perhaps all wiped out the families," the *Mayfield Daily Times* told its readers on June 27, 1921. "No more horrible incident has been written on the pages of Graves County history."

Tragedies

Soon after the blaze, a coroner's jury hastily convened in Mayfield, the county seat. The panel ruled that the Saturday night fire was foul play, but by a person or persons unknown. "To this good day, the rest of the story is a mystery," said the late Lon Carter Barton of Mayfield, Graves County's unofficial historian.

In the absence of hard evidence, theories abounded about the killer fire. Somebody said Lawrence was deranged and burned down the cabin. Other people believed the blaze was the evildoing of robbers or a neighbor who hated Lawrence. Natural causes—lighting or a meteorite—were proposed.

The *Times* stuck to the gruesome facts: "eleven charred bodies, burned to a fine crisp—[were] picked up from the glowing embers." Besides Lawrence, thirty-five, the death toll included his wife, Laura, and their three children—Fred, five; Ethlyn, four; and baby Ralph, just eleven months old. The other victims were Otis Drew, twenty-six; his wife, Ola, twenty-three; and their three children—Otis Jr., five; Harry, four; and "a three month old baby," as well as "Delma Drew, nephew of Otis Drew," the paper added.

Reportedly, the families often got together on Saturday nights to sing and play their fiddles, banjos and guitars. Nearby neighbors said they heard music coming from the log home before the fatal fire, which was discovered about midnight, the *Times* said.

"The first…on the scene declared the roof had not fallen in when they arrived," the paper reported.

> *Calling loudly…and receiving no answer they went to the Drew home which is nearby and finding no one there either, returned to the scene.*
>
> *One of them scaled an evergreen tree in front of the house and peered down through the smoke screen through the top of the door. It is said he recognized the form of Ernest Lawrence, lying face upward near the fireplace burning to a crisp.*
>
> *Another witness stated the screams of women and children [were] followed rapidly by six or seven shots. The shots, stated the witness, sounded like both pistol and gun shots.*

Two rifles, a pistol, a shotgun, an axe and an oilcan were picked out of the ashes, the *Times* said. "The finding of these weapons and the oil can is what led the coroner's jury to write foul play in their verdict after examining a dozen witnesses."

The pistol and shotgun had been fired, according to the paper. "So far no clews [*sic*] have been found that would lead to arrests or even strong suspicion," the *Times* added.

Leads went nowhere. Supposedly, somebody saw a prowler at the nearby Jones farm before the fire. Law officers turned up no such intruder.

In perhaps the most bizarre twist to the story, a stocky, well-dressed man showed up and confided in a relative of the Drew family that he was a U.S. Secret Service detective. Allegedly, the stranger whispered to the relative, "A sailor boy done it."

Authorities didn't believe the mystery man. They suspected he was "some one posing as a detective to make a 'show,'" the *Times* said. No sailor was ever found, and the stranger "absolutely disappeared as if the earth had swallowed him," according to the newspaper. "It is thought he stepped into a car and was whisked possibly to Paducah or Mayfield."

It seemed as if everybody had an idea of why the cabin burned down. Did a thief or thieves rob the families, then murder them in cold blood and burn the house to make good a getaway? That seemed unlikely. Apparently, neither family had much money.

Was the blaze the tragic result of a family quarrel? Ernest Drew and Otis Lawrence were brothers-in-law, having wed sisters Ola and Laura Riley. But there was no evidence of bad blood. To the contrary, the *Times* said, "each Saturday night it was the habit of one family to spend the night with the other and both being musicians it is generally known that the men were best of friends enjoying each other like brothers."

Another theory held that Ernest Drew suffered "fits of insanity" stemming from an old head injury. He finally went completely mad and set the fire, or so some people said.

Dr. W.S. Hargrove of Hickory flatly denied it. "He was a hard working married man," the physician told the *Times*. "And if a lick he had on the head ever gave him any trouble he never let it be known to me."

Lightning and a meteorite were ruled out. The night was clear. It was obvious, too, that nothing else hurtling from the heavens had caused the blaze.

Meanwhile, the rumor mill continued to grind as sheriff and police investigations stalled. A story circulated that a neighbor harbored a grudge against Ernest Lawrence, swore to kill him and all his kin—and did it.

No such vengeful neighbor was found. The *Times* said Lawrence had no known enemies.

But everybody agreed that the fire was no accident. If it had been, the argument went, why was nobody able to escape the fatal flames?

Delma Drew, fourteen, apparently came nearest to getting away. His fire-blackened body was found closest to the door, "heaped up in what looked like a crouching position," according to the *Times*. "It is presumed that he discovered the fire or in some other manner was trying to crawl to the door when overcome or met with foul play."

The other victims were in what had been the two front rooms of the cabin. Coroner O.M. Merritt and W.H. Fielder, a Mayfield undertaker, verified that there were eleven bodies. "After a careful search they were all identified," the *Times* said.

But the reported gunfire coming from the blazing house was never fully explained. Apparently, the bodies were burned so badly that it was impossible to tell if any of the victims had been shot. It is possible that the weapons went off as they burned up.

In any event, word of the tragedy quickly spread. Gawkers flocked to the cabin site. "Long streams of automobiles wended up a winding lane which leads to the Lawrence home," the *Times* reported on June 28, 1921.

The next day, the remains of all eleven victims were buried in a single coffin in the county seat cemetery in view of "hundreds of sympathizers," according to the *Times*.

> *The sight, one of the saddest ever seen in Graves County, and certainly the saddest sight since the civil war, was enough to make strong men cry. Two aged mothers, one had lost two sons and three grand children; another had lost six daughters and six grand children. Other relatives gathered in large numbers and as the casket was tenderly lowered to its last resting place wails of the stricken relatives could be heard piercing the peaceful quiet of beautiful Maplewood.*

Quiet has long since returned to the old burial ground and its only mass grave. A simple slab about four feet tall, the Lawrence-Drew tombstone does not stand out among the hundreds of other memorials, large or small, in solemn marble and polished granite.

Carved deeply in the stone, the epitaph is still legible. But a little metal sign in front of the marker also explains that this single grave contains the "remains of 11 persons buried in one coffin, Drew and Lawrence families, victims of housefire 1921."

"Greatest Cave Explorer Ever Known"

After four funerals and four burials in almost sixty-four years, Floyd Collins finally rests in peace at Mammoth Cave National Park.

Sand Cave entrance.

"A few people still ask about him," said Joe Duvall, a park ranger and cave guide.

Collins, the "Greatest Cave Explorer Ever Known," according to his tombstone, grabbed headlines worldwide in 1925 when he became trapped inside Sand Cave. He died despite heroic efforts to save him. By the time would-be rescuers reached Collins's lifeless body, "fifty reporters from sixteen big-city newspapers and film crews from six motion-picture studios had turned him into a popular martyr," wrote Michael Lesy in the October 1976 issue of *American Heritage* magazine. Collins's story inspired several magazine articles, books, a ballad, a movie and a musical.

Lesy called the scene outside Sand Cave "half circus, half revival meeting." Local entrepreneurs sold hot dogs, sandwiches, coffee and moonshine to thousands of curiosity-seekers who came to watch the rescuers. Governor William J. Fields sent the National Guard to keep order.

Collins was buried—presumably for the final time—in 1989 at Mammoth Cave Baptist Church Cemetery. The graveyard and the old wooden house of worship are inside the national park. Collins's remains were transferred from nearby Crystal Cave, where his coffin and tombstone were tourist attractions

Tragedies

from 1927 until 1961, when the National Park Service bought the cave and closed it.

"His grand-nephew, Donnie Collins, who lives in the area, wanted Floyd to finally have a decent burial," said Duvall, an authority on the storied spelunker. "Floyd is buried next to his mom."

The Greatest Cave Explorer hoped to discover or dynamite a passage from Sand Cave, owned by a neighbor, to the Great Crystal Cave, which belonged to the Collins family. "Floyd discovered Crystal Cave in 1917, but it was five miles from nowhere," Duvall said. Sand Cave is next to the main road leading to Mammoth Cave.

Collins's final resting place.

On January 30, 1925, Collins, a thirty-seven-year-old bachelor, was working alone in Sand Cave when he became pinned under a rock ledge in a narrow tunnel sixty feet below ground. He was found the next day. Floyd's brothers, Homer and Marshall, and a small army of volunteers worked for seventeen days to save him.

William "Skeets" Miller, a wiry little reporter for the *Courier-Journal*, wriggled into the damp, dark, cold, cramped cavern to interview Collins. He also brought Floyd food and tried to free him with a car jack.

Miller, who was only five feet tall and barely weighed one hundred pounds, became a story unto himself. The *Courier-Journal* headlined its man "Skeets the First," dubbing him "ruler of Cave City," the closest town to Mammoth Cave. "His stories about Floyd Collins won him a Pulitzer Prize," Duvall said.

With time running out and a fresh rockslide blocking the only passage leading to Collins, volunteers, including Muhlenberg County coal miners, desperately began digging a rescue shaft from the surface. When the tunnelers reached Collins on February 16, he was dead. He succumbed to starvation and exposure, Duvall said.

The miners announced that it would not be safe to try to get the body out, according to Duvall. "So Floyd was left buried in the cave, and the first funeral service was held at the entrance."

Afterward, Homer Collins hired some other Muhlenberg miners to retrieve the body. "They got Floyd out, but there was some speculation that the body wasn't his," Duvall said. "They positively identified him by his gold tooth, a bank deposit slip in his pocket and a photograph."

The family buried Collins next to the entrance to the Great Crystal Cave on April 26, 1925. "They were poor farmers and perhaps hoped to attract more tourists," Duvall said. "Anyway, they held another funeral service."

In 1927, Dr. Harry Thomas, a Horse Cave dentist, bought the Great Crystal Cave and renamed it Floyd Collins's Crystal Cave. He dug up Collins, put him inside the cave, added a tombstone and charged admission. Visitors could peer through a glass window in Collins's coffin and see the corpse, which was stolen in 1929 and recovered two days later along the Green River. Missing was the left leg—the one pinned in Sand Cave.

Meanwhile, some Collins kin had protested against putting Floyd's coffin on display just to make money. "But Dr. Thomas claimed that the cave was where Floyd would want to be," Duvall said. "Anyway, that was his third service—inside the cave."

Duvall said Collins's March 24, 1989 rites would likely be his last. "That service—number four—wasn't open to the media. Only people who could prove they were relatives of his were allowed to attend."

Sand Cave and Collins's grave—marked by the old brown tombstone Dr. Thomas had inside Crystal Cave—are both near the visitors' center and main entrance to Mammoth Cave. A boardwalk leads to the mouth of Sand Cave.

4
Gone but Not Forgotten

Upright Fellow

Willis P. Westray has been dead since 1860, but he's still on his feet near Lowes. He asked to be buried standing up with a bottle of whiskey in one hand and a hatchet or a brickbat in the other.

"Willis said he wanted to be ready for the devil," said the late Roy Lowe, whose family founded Lowes. "If the devil was friendly, they'd have a drink together. But if Satan wanted a fight, Willis had his hatchet or brickbat."

Lowe, who operated a local funeral home for many years, cited *A Glance Backwards for 100 Years Anniversary of the Centennial of Lowes*, a booklet the 1937 class of old Lowes High School wrote to celebrate the Graves County community's centennial.

Westray's tombstone and the cemetery where he was buried are long gone. But "Meet the Devil" was carved on the old grave marker, along with "Willis P. Westray/Born January 6, 1791/Died April 3, 1860/Wife—Sarah."

Explains the pamphlet, "As the story goes, Willis was a pretty bad actor, going out on sprees and getting drunk being a general habit with him. His wife, Sarah, was a good church member, however. Willis was often prayed for in church, but little good did this do."

Purportedly, Westray was in his cups when he made his funeral arrangements. He announced "in blunt statements that he wanted to meet the devil prepared or 'headlong' as he expressed it," the pamphlet says. "It was his wish to be buried standing up with a hatchet in one hand and a bottle of whiskey or a brickbat in the other."

The pamphlet suggests that Westray may have been joking:

> *But it was taken seriously by his family. Willis' grave was round, about six feet deep and lined with bricks. He was buried standing up and the hatchet was put in the coffin with him, but he did not have it in his hand. There is no record in the minds of the old settlers who heard the story from their fathers as to whether or not the brickbat and the whiskey are in the coffin.*

Sarah Westray was interred next to her husband, but apparently horizontally, according to the pamphlet. Her tombstone disappeared, too.

For years, a locust thicket hid the graves. But the trees and brush were cleared away, apparently along with the Westrays' grave markers.

"That Other Guy Was a Copycat"

Willis P. Westray is not the only western Kentuckian buried standing up.

"Joe Puntney was too—and he was the first," Gene Stewart said of his wife Fay's great-great-grandfather. "That other guy was a copycat."

Perhaps a decade or two before the Civil War, Puntney was buried upright on a sandy hill near the Mississippi River in Carlisle County. "It was his request that when he died, he was to be buried standing so he could see his livestock down below," said Stewart, who lives in La Center, in adjacent Ballard County.

Puntney owned considerable property next to a bend in the river. He arrived in the 1820s aboard a flatboat, according to *History and Memories of Carlisle County* by Ran Graves.

Ultimately, the bend was named for Puntney, who built a lively river trade, which included selling wood for fuel to steamboats. The hill where Puntney was buried also contains the remains of some steamboat passengers who died on the nearby river, according to Graves.

"The captain had to get rid of them, so he would have a crude coffin made" and force his deckhands, mainly slaves, to pile the bodies into oxcarts and carry them from Puntney's bend to the cemetery, the author added.

A few of the old stones remain atop the pointy, steep-sided, oak-studded hill, one of several such knobs that local settlers dubbed "the pints." Graves said a number of the hills were also graveyards, "but they have been neglected for 75 or 80 years and nothing remains."

Gone but Not Forgotten

Puntney's home and freight house are long gone. Only farmland stretches to Puntney's Bend.

Graves mentioned the story of Puntney's unusual interment. "There is a rumor that the first Puntney was buried there standing up facing the bottom, so he could see his horses, cattle and hogs pass going in and out of the bottoms."

"The Strange Procession Which Never Moves"

A single tombstone wouldn't do for Henry G. Wooldridge, a wealthy eccentric who enjoyed horses and hunting. The Mayfield man figured eighteen was more like it.

"They call it all 'the strange procession which never moves,'" said Martha Babb, former local chamber of commerce tourism director. "People from all over the United States and Canada, too, stop and ask about the Wooldridge Monuments."

"The Strange Procession Which Never Moves."

Wooldridge is buried in old Maplewood Cemetery beneath two statues of himself, one afoot, the other on horseback. The stone Henrys are kept company for eternity by statues of his mother, four brothers, three sisters, two great-nieces, two dogs, a deer and a fox.

Wooldridge's earthly remains are in a simple, slab-sided stone crypt. A tall shaft in his honor makes eighteen monuments on a fifteen- by twenty-five-foot plot. "Mr. Wooldridge is the only one buried there," Babb said. "That's what's so strange about it."

Wooldridge died on May 30, 1899, at age seventy-seven. He ordered the statues in the 1890s.

The late Nathan Yates explained that Wooldridge wanted a "memorial… that would be different from that of the prosaic type appearing in most cemeteries."

Author of a little booklet titled *The World Famous Wooldridge Monuments*, Yates added that Wooldridge designed "an open air Hall of Fame, where, for all time, the figures of himself, members of his family, and the animals he loved would be preserved in enduring stone."

The standing statue of Wooldridge was carved of marble in Italy and shipped to Mayfield at a cost of $1,000. City stonemasons carved three statues; William Lydon of Paducah sculpted the rest.

Lydon used an eleven-ton chunk of Indiana quarried stone. The equestrian statue weighed 2.5 tons, and the Illinois Central Railroad dispatched an air brake–equipped flatcar from St. Louis to haul the stone horse and rider to Mayfield.

Allegedly, a Mayfield drunk staggered by the rail yard just before the train pulled out. Needing a lift back to town, he climbed on the horse and rode home in style, or so the story goes.

Other legends surround the statues. "Mr. Wooldridge was a bachelor, but supposedly he was engaged to a girl who died," Babb said. "People said one of the little statues is his fiancée as a child."

Years ago, souvenir hunters broke the ears off the deer and took the dogs' tails. A fence was built around the monuments to keep vandals at bay.

But the barrier could not prevent major damage in January 2009, when Mayfield suffered the worst ice storm in western Kentucky history. Caked with heavy ice, the limb of a huge oak tree snapped off and smashed several of the statues, all of which have since been painstakingly repaired.

The Wooldridge Monuments have achieved a degree of national recognition. Actor Jack Palance once came to town to be filmed at the monuments for an episode of the *Ripley's Believe It or Not* TV show.

The monuments also appeared briefly in the 1989 movie *In Country*. Starring Bruce Willis and Emily Lloyd, most of the film was shot in and around Mayfield in 1988.

"Back Home"

Irvin S. Cobb was a famous journalist, fiction writer and humorist. But some critics say a letter containing his funeral instructions and views on organized religion ranks among his best works.

Cobb said he didn't want to be sent to his reward via "the so-Christian burial service which, in view of the language employed in it, I regard as one of the most cruel and paganish things inherited by our forebears from our remote pagan ancestors."

Cobb's letter grabbed headlines nationwide. It "was reprinted, attacked, applauded, and dissected…in waves of editorials and letters to the editor," according to *Irvin S. Cobb* by Anita Lawson. "The articles and letters which praised him soon outnumbered those which criticized him."

Many people who condemned the letter missed the point of Cobb's irreverence, said Andrew Halford, a Cobb scholar who taught English at West Kentucky Community and Technical College in Paducah, Cobb's hometown. "It was satire," Halford said. "Cobb was having fun."

Cobb composed his last rites in December 1943, knowing he was mortally ill. He died on March 10, 1944, in New York City at age sixty-seven. He was buried in Paducah's old Oak Grove Cemetery.

Born in Paducah in 1876, Cobb moved to New York in 1904 and became a newspaper reporter. He wound up at the *Evening Herald*, where Cobb's "reputation rose dramatically, bolstered by his coverage of the murder trials of socialite Harry Thaw in 1907 and 1908," Lawson wrote in *The Kentucky Encyclopedia*.

Cobb also began to write humorous fiction, mostly drawn from his childhood in Paducah, a historic old Ohio River town. The *Saturday Evening Post* published several of Cobb's stories, and he joined the magazine in 1912, Lawson added.

Cobb covered World War I in Europe for the *Post* and became one of America's most famous combat correspondents. After the war, he worked for *Cosmopolitan* and wrote screenplays in Hollywood, where he acted in a half dozen movies. He also had his own nationally syndicated radio show.

All along, Cobb wrote numerous novels and short stories, often set in Paducah and usually with a humorous theme. His autobiography, *Exit Laughing*, was published three years before his death.

Irvin S. Cobb. *Courtesy of the Library of Congress.*

Gone but Not Forgotten

Cobb's grave site in Paducah.

Cobb, too, was a master storyteller and popular after-dinner speaker. However, he wished not to be buried in "the regalia of that craft…a tail-coat with white tie and artificial pearl studs." Cobb explained that once he was gone, he'd "be done with after-dinner speaking forever."

Cobb mailed the letter with his funeral instructions to the *Paducah Sun-Democrat* with strict orders that it "be kept, with the seal unbroken, in a safe or safe deposit box in the custody of the [newspaper]…management." His wishes were honored.

After the *Sun-Democrat* published the letter, editors telegraphed it to the *New York Times*, *Daily News* and *Herald-Tribune*. The Associated Press and United Press International dispatched the letter to newspapers coast to coast.

Cobb requested that his "body be wrapped in a plain sheet of cloth and placed in an inexpensive container and immediately cremated—without any formality or special ceremony." Cobb warned that his ghost would "ha'nt" anybody who "tries to insert me into one of those dismal numbers run up by the undertaker's dressmaking department."

Cobb noted that cremation would remove the "need for pallbearers, as the trade term goes. Pallbearers are another surviving relic of heathen practices."

He guessed that his ashes "properly rendered down…shouldn't much more than fill a Mason's fruit jar." He suggested one of two Paducah poker pals "as a dependable custodian of my mortal remains on the trip to the burying-ground." Both gents, he recalled, "could cuddle to their bosoms three of a kind in a dollar limit game."

Cobb again asked his family not to wear "the bogus habiliments of so-called mourning. Folds of black crepe never ministered to the memory of the departed; they only made the wearers unhappy and self-conscious."

He urged that his memorial be just a dogwood tree, fertilized by his remains. Such a tree shades his grave.

But he gave his relatives permission to mark his burial place, too, with "a slab of plain Kentucky limestone set flat in the kindly earth, or a rugged natural boulder of Southern granite." They chose the latter, adding "Back Home" as an epitaph.

In addition, Cobb asked friends to donate money to a local nondenominational charity rather than buying flowers for him. He said Christmas berries and cedar boughs were suitable adornments for his final resting place if he died in winter. He wanted "leafy boughs from native hickories or hackberries or wild crab-apples if it be in other seasons."

Cobb requested "no long faces and no show of grief at the burying ground." Though a life member of the Paducah Elks' Lodge, he asked that the Elks' burial service not be read because, "like most burial programs, it needs editing."

He requested that choirs from African American churches sing "Swing Low, Sweet Chariot" and "Deep River." While segregation was rigid in the Paducah of 1944, Cobb "took up the cause of racial tolerance" after World War I, Lawson wrote in *The Kentucky Encyclopedia*. In 1922, Cobb denounced the Ku Klux Klan as "the masked brotherhood of bigotry, bravado and bunk" in a guest editorial he wrote for the *Paducah News Democrat*, where he was managing editor in his youth.

Cobb said he would allow the reading of the Twenty-third Psalm at his last rites. It was his Presbyterian mother's favorite scripture, he explained. Cobb said he also enjoyed the familiar Old Testament passage best because

> *it contains no charnel words, no morbid mouthings about corruption and decay and, being mercifully without creed or dogma, carries no threat of eternal hell fire for those parties we do not like, no direct promise of a heaven which, if one may judge by the people who are surest of going there, must be a powerfully dull place, populated to a considerable and*

uncomfortable degree by prigs, time-servers and unpleasantly aggressive individuals. Hell might have a worse climate but undoubtedly the company is sprightlier.

Cobb explained that his ideal religion "would combine the dignity and the beauty of the Romanist ritual with certain other ingredients; the good taste and the ability of the Unitarians and Episcopalians—a trait not too common to some of the Evangelical groups—to mind their own business. (I'm proud that I never set myself up to be My Brother's Keeper, having been sufficiently occupied by the job of being my own keeper.)"

He added:

To these add the noble ethics and the splendid tolerance expressed in Reformed Judaism; the sturdy independence and the good business principles of the Mormons; the gentle humility and orderly humanity of the Quakers, plus the militant zeal and unselfish devotion of those Shock Troops of the Lord— The Salvation Army, who fight in the trenches of Sin's No Man's Land to reclaim the tortured souls and clothe the naked bodies of those whom the rest of a snobbish world forgot. If, based on this combination, there was a determination to practice the sectless preachments and the teaching of Jesus Christ who was the first true gentleman of recorded history and the greatest gentleman that ever lived, I might not have joined the fold, but certainly I'd have stood on the side lines and cheered for it.

Whatever Cobb meant by his impiety, it had one result that would have made him happy, wrote Lawson, a former English professor at Murray State University: "Editorialists and citizens commenting on his death were forced to deal with his opinions, not merely with his jokes."

"THE SLEEPING PROPHET"

Did Edgar Cayce, the celebrated psychic, foretell the death of President Woodrow Wilson? If he so soothsaid, it was an easy call, according to historian and writer Ron Bryant.

"Wilson had suffered a massive stroke," Bryant said. "It's a miracle he was still alive."

Supposedly, Cayce, who is buried in Hopkinsville, also warned Wilson that the Treaty of Versailles would fail to pass the U.S. Senate. "Anyone who

Cayce's grave site in Hopkinsville.

had read the newspapers or listened to talk on the streets knew the treaty was in trouble," said Bryant, manager at the Waveland Museum State Historic Site in Lexington.

Born near Hopkinsville, the Christian County seat, in 1877, Cayce became a world-famous seer. He "used his reputed gift of extra sensory perception, including medical diagnosis, to better man's understanding of God's purpose for him here on earth," claims a state historical marker at the entrance to Riverside Cemetery, where Cayce slumbers eternally.

Gone but Not Forgotten

The western Kentuckian died at Virginia Beach, Virginia, in 1945. He was sixty-seven.

Cayce is said to have given more than fourteen thousand psychic "readings," all while he was in a sleep-like trance. Powerful politicians, church leaders, business tycoons and other celebrities sought the services of "the Sleeping Prophet."

He "read" for inventors Thomas Edison and Nikola Tesla, composers Irving Berlin and George Gershwin and actress Gloria Swanson, according to *Edgar Cayce: An American Prophet* by Sidney D. Kirkpatrick. "The concerned mother of Ernest Hemingway…consulted Cayce about her son's writing career," the author added.

Cayce purportedly "was asked to give medical readings for President Wilson" in "late November or early December of 1920," Kirkpatrick wrote. Wilson "had suffered a stroke [in October 1919] while campaigning for the ill-fated League of Nations and was confined to a wheelchair," he explained. The president's doctor "had given up all hope for Wilson's recovery," the author also wrote.

According to Dave Kahn, a longtime Cayce aide, Colonel Will Starling, a Hopkinsville native, united the president and the prognosticator. Starling, an ex-pitcher for the Hopkinsville Moguls baseball team, was a secret service agent assigned to guard Wilson.

Cayce had given readings for Starling. They were old friends, according to Kirkpatrick.

"I did not see the reading given," Kirkpatrick quoted Kahn. "But as I understand, it described the president's condition and foretold that his time was limited and that he would not get well."

Wilson lived until 1924.

It is not clear if Cayce "read" for Wilson, a Democrat, about the Treaty of Versailles, which the president helped draft after World War I. In 1920, the Republican-majority Senate rejected the treaty over the League of Nations, which Wilson considered the pact's most important provision.

"Cayce definitely had some interesting 'visions,'" Bryant said. "But his place in history is secured in a more *Ripley's Believe It or Not* genre, rather than in fact."

5
Towns and Their Roots

"There Are Several Veins of Ore, and a Bed a Foot Thick"

Early in the Civil War, Union and Confederate brass recognized the military importance of Columbus, where steep dirt bluffs known as the Iron Banks tower over the Mississippi River.

The Confederates got there first. They dug deep trenches on the high ground, planted big cannons and dragged a heavy chain across the river to block Yankee gunboats. Some of the trenches and the anchor used to fasten the chain to the Kentucky shore are featured attractions at Columbus-Belmont State Park.

But almost three centuries before, the famous French explorer Jacques Marquette saw potential in the same high ground, part of a rolling bluff line that starts upriver at Wickliffe and stretches to Columbus and beyond. But mining, not military matters, was on Marquette's mind, said Paducah historian and author John Robertson.

Marquette and his young companion, Louis Joliet, marked the spot on their map as the *mine de fer*, or iron mine. The two figured they had happened upon a rich deposit of iron ore. "As it turned out, they hadn't," said Robertson, who taught history for many years at West Kentucky Community and Technical College. "But the 'Iron Banks,' a derivative of the name they gave the bluffs, survives."

Marquette, a Jesuit priest, and Joliet had left from French-held Lake Michigan in May 1673, with five men aboard two birch bark canoes. Their task was to explore the Mississippi River. "People think of Daniel Boone as among the earliest Europeans to set foot in Kentucky," Robertson said. "But Marquette and Joliet were here long before him."

The French explorers discovered the *mine de fer* after they paddled past the nearby junction of the Mississippi and the "Ouabouskigou," which Marquette described as the river that flowed "from the lands of the East." The Ouabouskigou is the Ohio River, Robertson said.

Marquette's account of his historic journey was recorded in *The Jesuit Relations*, a series of books about the travels of French Jesuit missionaries in America in the seventeenth and eighteenth centuries.

Marquette credited one of the five boatmen with spying the "iron mine" in earthen "cliffs" beside the river's edge. "There are several veins of ore, and a bed a foot thick, and one sees large masses of it united with Pebbles," Marquette wrote. He added that the bluffs were made of "a sticky earth… of three different colors—purple, violet, and Red. The water in which the latter is washed assumes a bloody tinge. There is also very heavy red sand."

Exploring ashore, Marquette decided to test the iron content in the sand by rubbing a handful of grains on his canoe paddle. The paddle, he wrote, "was dyed with its color—so deeply that the water could not wash it away during the 15 days while I used it for paddling."

Still visible in the bluffs are bits of iron ore, reddish sand and pudding stone, Marquette's masses of ore "united with Pebbles." "The Iron Banks probably looked very much the same to Marquette as they do today," Robertson said.

Except for a metal historical marker in Columbus that says the Iron Banks were "so named by early French explorers," there are no other memorials linking Columbus to their famous voyage. The explorers reached the mouth of the Arkansas River before returning to Canada.

But about fifteen miles upriver at Wickliffe, close to where the Ohio and Mississippi join, another historical marker on U.S. Highway 51 says that the Frenchmen "stopped on this bank in 1673, according to *The Jesuit Relations*."

Indeed, Marquette wrote that the explorers encountered Native Americans evidently determined to fight. He admitted he was mistaken.

"They were as frightened as we were," Marquette explained, "and what we took for a signal for a battle was an invitation that they gave us to draw near, that they might give us food. We therefore landed, and entered their Cabins, where they offered us meat from wild cattle [buffalo] and bear's grease, with white plums, which are very good." The historical marker says the Europeans "were feasted by the Indians."

"What He Had Actually Done Was Prime the Well"

A dry well and twenty-four hours stood between William Hudspeth and his dream of a county seat sprouting on his property in pioneer south central Kentucky.

For days, his well stood empty. Then one morning, it suddenly brimmed with cold, clear water.

A miracle? "Not exactly," said Sue Groves Cooper, a former Simpson County archivist. "But the story is pretty well known in the county."

According to the tale, Franklin, the Simpson County seat, would have grown up someplace else if not for a Hudspeth hornswaggle. "You might say he tried to put one over on the people," said Cooper, who now lives in Antioch, Tennessee.

The yarn, recounted in old county history books, unravels in 1819, shortly after the legislature created Simpson County on the Kentucky-Tennessee state line. The state appointed three commissioners to select a site for the seat. "They wanted it to be where there was a good supply of water," Cooper said.

Commissioners Samuel Burrell of Barren County, John Cross of Christian County and Richard B. Dallahan of Butler County narrowed the choice to three locations: Ditmore's Ford on Drakes Creek, a tract that became the old county fairgrounds north of Franklin and Hudspeth's property.

The Hudspeth holding was about 1.5 miles from Drakes Creek. "Evidently, the commissioners liked his land the best, but they were concerned about water," Cooper said.

Hudspeth agreed to dig a well. He assured the commissioners that it would provide for a well-watered county seat.

But the well yielded only dirt and limestone rock. Hudspeth ordered the well dug deeper, but to no avail.

"Finally, the commissioners told him he had one more day to strike water," Cooper said.

Hudspeth hurriedly hatched a hoax. He waited until nightfall before recruiting a secret bucket brigade from among his slaves. Their orders: march on Drakes Creek and don't come back empty-bucketed, or so the story goes.

Hudspeth's well site, Franklin.

All night, the covert caravan trekked back and forth to the creek bank. Bucket by bucket, the well was filled to the top.

After dawn, a happy Hudspeth greeted the commissioners at the well. "They announced that Franklin would be built on his land," Cooper said.

Hudspeth left the new county, ending up in Missouri, according to Cooper. But he didn't depart astride a rail or sporting a new suit of tar and feathers.

"What he had actually done was prime the well," Cooper said. "In fact, the well turned out to be Franklin's water supply until about the time of the Civil War."

While it hasn't quenched a thirst in more than a century, the old well still stands on the south side of the court square in Franklin. "In the 1970s, the local Junior Historical Society built a little wooden well house over it," Cooper said.

Painted rusty red, the well house is near the courthouse and next to a historical marker that tells the story of Hudspeth's well. The plaque says Franklin was surveyed in 1819 and was "made county seat by Legislature, Nov. 1820."

Princeton Sprang from the Big Spring

William Prince's old tavern is long gone, but his other watering hole still gushes cold and clear in Big Spring Park.

"He was a good businessman," said the late Sam Steger, a historian in Princeton, which was named for the pioneer tavern keeper. "Three old pioneer trails crossed here. It was an ideal place to start a tavern."

And a town, he added.

First trod by buffalo and later by Native Americans and white settlers, the Saline, Varmint and Eddy Traces converged at the Big Spring, where Princeton began. "The Saline Trace started near Nashville," Steger said. "It branched north of the Big Spring and crossed the Ohio River into Illinois at Golconda and Cave-In-Rock." The shorter Varmint Trace led west from the Big Spring to the Cumberland River. Also called the Palmyra-Princeton Trace, the Eddy Trace began near Palmyra, Tennessee, and ended in Illinois.

A South Carolina native and Revolutionary War veteran, Prince migrated to the Big Spring in 1798. Settling on two hundred acres given him for war service, Prince constructed Shandy Hall, a two-story stone house that doubled as a backwoods inn. "It was said that he built firing ports in the walls in case of Indian attacks," Steger said.

The house stood in what is now downtown Princeton until about the 1830s, Steger said. "Supposedly, when they tore it down, they broke up the walls for paving stones and used them in early Princeton streets."

The Big Spring gushes from the base of a twenty-foot limestone ledge a block south of the courthouse in Princeton, the Caldwell County seat. It is the featured attraction in a little park built in the 1960s and maintained by a local garden club. A pair of historical markers tells about Shandy Hall and about the Cherokees who camped at the spring in 1838 on the Trail of Tears.

Princeton's Big Spring.

Steger said that in pioneer days, settlers used the landmark spring for water and for keeping butter, cheese and eggs fresh. An early doctor also tapped into the Big Spring for water to nurture his plants.

The physician discovered that the spring actually flowed from a cave that is about a mile long. "He was a really crafty old fellow," Steger said. "When he found that the cave ran near his home, he sunk a shaft down to it and used the water to keep his greenhouse from freezing in wintertime."

In the 1930s, a local engineer with the Works Progress Administration, part of President Franklin Roosevelt's New Deal program for fighting the Depression, explored Big Springs Cave, according to Steger. "He found a large underground lake at the end."

Steger also said that the Big Spring indirectly furnished Princeton's first name. "The community was called Eddy Grove because the spring is the head of Eddy Creek, which empties into the Cumberland."

According to one of the historical markers, the settlement was named Princetown and made the county seat in 1817. The name was shortened to Princeton the next year, according to the sign, which also says that the town "was situated on 50-acre donation of Prince heirs."

Towns and Their Roots

Fancy Farm Was Named for a Fancy Farm

A fancy farm inspired Fancy Farm.

In 1843, a U.S. postal inspector named the Graves County hamlet synonymous with the state's most famous political picnic.

Kentucky is a fertile field for unusual place names. Fancy Farm, for instance, is not too far from Monkey's Eyebrow and Possum Trot. Dublin, Cuba and Moscow are nearby.

The pre–Civil War postal inspector was impressed with the community that became Fancy Farm, especially the farm of John Peebles, his host, or so the story goes. Peebles wanted to be postmaster, according to Father Charles A. Haeseley, who was a longtime pastor in Fancy Farm. Founded by descendants of colonial Maryland Catholics who fled west to escape religious persecution, Fancy Farm is a Catholic enclave in Bible Belt Protestant western Kentucky.

According to Haeseley's writings, Peebles "was noted for taking pride in the appearance of his home and farm, and employed every means of the

St. Jerome Church, Fancy Farm.

then-existing conditions permitted to enhance the beauty and attractiveness of his property."

Pastor from 1888 to 1920, Haeseley also wrote, "Whilst being a guest of Mr. Peebles the Post Office inspector was requested to suggest an appropriate name for the new office. In a compliment to Mr. Peebles as an agriculturalist he proposed 'Fancy Farm' as a most suitable name. So the promising infant was christened, and has ever since retained the same."

The Fancy Farm post office opened on March 15, 1843, with Peebles in charge. The community has grown to about three hundred residents, although thousands more crowd Fancy Farm every August for picnics that feature pork barbecue and political speechmaking, both spicy hot.

Fancy Farm is home to one of Kentucky's smallest post offices, a 1960s-vintage red brick building. But customers are not just locals. Occasionally, the postmaster gets mail from stamp collectors all over the country. Seeking a Fancy Farm postmark, they enclose stamped, self-addressed envelopes.

"A Thousand Pleasant Memories"

Long before Lake Barkley, Charles Anderson dreamed that Kuttawa would become a famous health resort.

A Kentucky-born ex-governor of Ohio, Anderson founded Kuttawa in the 1870s atop Lyon County mineral springs that he hoped would gush everlasting prosperity.

"A lot of people did come to Kuttawa to drink the water," Odell Walker said. "It was popular until about World War II, but afterward it went into decline."

Kuttawa is a small resort community on Lake Barkley, created in the 1960s when the U.S. Army Corps of Engineers straddled the Cumberland River with Barkley Dam. Evidently unknown to most tourists, the Kuttawa springs still pump cold, clear water into the nearby lake at a purported 135,000 gallons every twenty-four hours.

Anderson, according to Walker's book *Profiles of the Past*, hoped "that his beloved Kuttawa and surrounding area would become a resort similar to French Lick in Indiana or Hot Springs, Arkansas."

Early Kuttawa boosters touted a Louisville chemist's 1890 report that claimed the spring water "could be used advantageously in the treatment of diseases and functional disorders of the stomach, liver and kidneys." Walker doubts the water can cure anything.

Towns and Their Roots

"It's good water, but in the old days, people believed mineral water had medicinal value," he said. "So anybody who had a spring called it a 'mineral spring.'"

Kuttawa never rivaled French Lick or Hot Springs. But Walker said that enough visitors came to town to support a small hotel. Some guests were former Confederate soldiers.

Anderson was a Yankee colonel in the Civil War, but many ex-Rebels held reunions at the springs. A popular speaker was Congressman W.J. Stone, a Lyon Countian who lost a leg fighting for the South. His wife, Cornelia, upstaged him at one Confederate conclave when she led the gray-bearded old gray coats in blood-curdling Rebel yells, Walker said.

In the 1920s, the Kuttawa Mineral Springs Co. expanded the hotel into a resort that boasted holiday cabins, baseball diamonds, tennis and croquet courts, a barbecue restaurant and a swimming pool.

At the same time, the springs started attracting big camp meeting revivals in the summer. "I remember going to one in a farm wagon," Walker said. "My mother fixed us a basket lunch and spread it on a quilt, and my older brother got a gallon jug of fresh water from the spring. We had a big time."

Evangelists such as the Reverend Howard S. Williams of Mississippi saved souls in a big pavilion. "It looked like a pole barn," Walker said. "There was an old farm dinner bell, and they rang it when services were ready to start."

Walker said camp meetings usually lasted about two weeks. "The Sunday in the middle was homecoming. People who had roots here and who had gone off to find jobs came back if they could."

It was said that when Williams preached, he packed the pavilion. Williams, who drove a shiny Lincoln car, confessed that before he came to Jesus, he sinned regularly as a newspaperman and gambler.

Williams's sometime song leader was an ex-vaudeville piano player named Moody. Reputedly, Moody made church music on an old handsaw and plinked out hymns on partly filled water glasses.

The Kuttawa Mineral Springs resort is long gone. There are reminders close by in old Mineral Springs Road and a new Kuttawa Springs subdivision.

Apparently, the only relic of Anderson's dream is a low concrete cover built to protect the springs in the 1930s. But it disappears under water when the lake rises.

"The Kuttawa Mineral Springs was a favorite spot for couples," Walker wrote in his book. "Sometimes several couples would meet there and sit on the concrete spring top…Other times a couple would park under the trees to spend a few minutes…and maybe snatch a kiss or two and a hug. For all who were ever touched by the magic of Kuttawa Springs, there must remain a thousand pleasant memories."

6
REALLY HIDDEN HISTORY

THE BLACK JACK JOG

There's a little pie-shaped wedge in the state line south of Franklin, and some say it's the work of pie-eyed surveyors.

"They were supposedly after some whiskey when they ran the line," Sue Groves Cooper said. "The story is unsubstantiated. But it's a good piece of county folklore."

Elsewhere, the Kentucky-Tennessee boundary runs straight for miles. But in Simpson County, Kentucky, it wedges into Tennessee. A green metal marker framed by a blue Welcome to Kentucky sign tells motorists on U.S. 31W that they've arrived in the Bluegrass State at a spot known locally as Black Jack Jog. Explains the marker:

> *The Simpson County jog in Kentucky-Tennessee boundary was error of Dr. Thomas Walker's 1780 survey party. Luke Munsell and James Bright resurveyed region fifty years later, but the controversy continued until survey by Austin P. Cox and Benjamin Peebles in 1858–1859. This stone-marked line set official boundary between the two states and ended an 80-yr. dispute.*

The jog forms a shallow triangle whose apex is about a mile south of its almost six-mile-long base. Allegedly, the border bulge resulted when a

Black Jack Jog marker.

pioneer landowner successfully schemed to shove the line south in 1780. He used a barrel of booze as bait, or so it was claimed.

"His name was Sanford Duncan, and he owned a stagecoach stop near the border," Cooper said. "Trouble was, the line evidently ran through his property."

Duncan reasoned that while land couldn't be moved, boundaries could. He plotted for the day surveyors would show up.

Really Hidden History

They did in 1780, when Kentucky was still part of Virginia and Tennessee belonged to North Carolina. In pre-statehood days, the Kentucky-Tennessee border country was wild, sparsely settled and dotted only here and there by rough log cabins.

Walker and his surveyors discovered that Sanford Duncan owned the one fine home in the region. He invited them to stay the weekend, plying them with soft beds, rich food and all the hooch they could drink.

When it was time to go to work Monday morning, the crew hinted that surveying was hard, thirsty work. The obliging Duncan rolled out a barrel of his best corn liquor, plopping it down under a big tree at the edge of his property on Tennessee turf.

Duncan let it be known that he wouldn't mind if the state line just happened to detour around the whiskey barrel. The surveyors happily complied, or so the story went. After draining the barrel, they shot the line back toward Kentucky and stayed the course ever afterward.

There's no proof that the story is true. But the Simpson County entry in *The Kentucky Encyclopedia* says only that one explanation for the bent boundary is "the hospitality of a local landowner who persuaded the surveyors to allow his land to remain north of the border."

Elsewhere, the compendium says the hiccup in the state line was the honest mistake of sober surveyors. They simply strayed off course from a marked beech tree on the bank of Drakes Creek, the *Encyclopedia* says. "When… Walker arrived from Nashville and discovered the error, the surveyors reset their compass rather than go back and correct their error. A black jack oak was marked at the apex of the jog."

Anyway, a few Nashville hot bloods probably were glad some Kentucky territory ended up a tad closer to the Tennessee capital. A remote section of Duncan's land known as "Linkumpinch" became a famous out-of-state dueling ground for Tennesseans with affairs of honor to settle.

If surveyors found Sanford Duncan accommodating, duelists may have, too. Some of them stayed at his inn, which still stands but as a private home. Another historical marker denotes the old dwelling. Guests possibly included Sam Houston, who wounded General William White at Linkumpinch in 1826, a year before dueling ceased in Simpson County, according to *The Kentucky Encyclopedia*.

"It's a Good Story, the Kind of Folklore that Makes History Interesting"

Did Thomas Jefferson really want Columbus to be the capital of the United States?

"The old folks said that he stood on the bluff overlooking the Mississippi River and declared that the capital should be built here," said the late Lucille Owings, a local historian. "I've also heard it was James Madison. Anyway, for years, they called the spot 'Capitol Hill.'"

An old historical marker in town claims, "COLUMBUS WAS PROPOSED AS THE NATION'S CAPITAL AFTER THE WAR OF 1812."

But John Robertson doubts Jefferson, Madison or anybody else in Washington wanted Columbus for a new capital. But he agreed that earlier generations of Columbus dwellers vowed that "Congress, by only one vote, decided to keep the capital in Washington and not move it to Columbus."

Robertson said Robert Summers, post–Civil War editor of the *Columbus Dispatch*, apparently started the legend of Columbus as the almost capital of the United States.

"In 1869, Summers began running a 'card' in his paper that extolled the virtues of Columbus and suggested that customers ought to support the *Dispatch* to further their own interests and ensure the growth of the city," Robertson explained.

But Robertson said Summers's "card" held that President James Madison, not his friend Jefferson, "stood on the bluff at Columbus and proclaimed, 'Here, some day, will stand the capital of the nation.'"

Summers provided no evidence of a Columbus-Madison connection. But Robertson suspects that the editor's local boosterism was based on proposals by some midwestern newspaper editors and influential politicians to move the capital west, the direction in which the country was growing.

John A. Logan, an Illinois congressman, senator, vice-presidential candidate and plainspoken ex-Yankee general, supported

Thomas Jefferson. *Courtesy of the Library of Congress.*

Really Hidden History

The bluffs at Columbus.

a new western capital. Logan complained that even after the Rebels had been whipped in the Civil War, it was "obvious that a disloyal element exists in the city of Washington."

At various times, St. Louis, Missouri; Fort Leavenworth, Kansas; and Columbus, Nebraska, were touted as new capital sites. "In October 1869, a National Capital Convention met in St. Louis to consider the removal of the national capital to the Mississippi Valley," Robertson said. "Several other commercial conventions were held."

One gathering in Iowa wanted the capital shifted to St. Louis.

Robertson also said that another version of the legend has Columbus being proposed as a replacement capital after the British burned Washington during the War of 1812. "But there is no proof that Jefferson or Madison visited Columbus," he added.

Nationally known historians have weighed in against Columbus as a proposed capital site. In his 1993 book, *Columbus, Kentucky as the Nation's Capital: Legend or Reality?*, Texan Allen Anthony quoted some famous Jefferson scholars, all of whom doubted Columbus was ever considered as the nation's capital.

"I can't imagine where such a story could have come from," said Professor Merrill D. Peterson of the University of Virginia. "Jefferson was an ardent proponent of the Grand Columbian Federal City, Washington, D.C., and never to my knowledge advocated another national capital."

Professor Eugene R. Sheridan of Princeton University told Anthony, "There is simply no evidence that Columbus, Kentucky, was ever considered as a site for the national capital, either by the Continental Congress, the federal Congress or by Thomas Jefferson." Sheridan added that Jefferson "could never have been in Columbus."

Even so, Hickman Countians have had fun with the capital legend. The late Virginia Jewell, a local newspaper columnist, once illustrated a story on the subject with a doctored photo showing the U.S. Capitol perched on a Columbus bluff top.

"It's a good story, the kind of folklore that makes history interesting," Owings said with a chuckle. "But it ought to be taken with a grain of salt."

"Swans by the Hundreds, and White as Rich Cream"

It was supposed to be an uneventful stop on a keelboat trip to old St. Genevieve in America's new Louisiana Territory.

But the weary wayfarer could hardly believe his eyes after he slogged through sloughs and pushed past a curtain of tall cottonwood trees to the lake near where the Ohio and Mississippi Rivers merge.

He beheld "swans by the hundreds, and white as rich cream, either dipping their black bills in the water, or stretching out one leg on its surface, or gently floating along." The traveler and his Shawnee hunting companions quickly bagged more than fifty of the big birds, "whose skins were intended for the ladies in Europe."

But the hunter was better known for stalking birds with a paintbrush than a gun. Still, John James Audubon recalled his 1810 shooting expedition to Swan Lake as one of his greatest adventures.

Apparently, America's famous naturalist and wildlife artist named Swan Lake, a cypress and buttonbush-ringed pool near Wickliffe, the Ballard County seat.

The trumpeter swans are long gone from the three-hundred-acre state-owned lake, where it is illegal to hunt wildfowl. To Audubon, who ran general stores in Louisville and Henderson, Swan Lake was a happy hunting ground.

Really Hidden History

Swan Lake.

"He and his partner, Ferdinand Rozier, had been in Henderson for about six months when they set out for St. Genevieve," said Don Boarman, retired curator at John James Audubon State Park in Henderson, 175 miles up the Ohio from Swan Lake.

Audubon and Rozier hoped business might be better in St. Genevieve, which French settlers founded on the Mississippi below St. Louis. So they shoved off from Henderson in cold, snowy December 1810, their keelboat laden with "three hundred barrels of whiskey, sundry drygoods, and powder," Audubon wrote. News of an icebound Mississippi forced a temporary halt on the Illinois shore a short distance from the Ohio's mouth.

Some Shawnees were camping close by, and Audubon asked if he could go along on a hunt to the "large lake opposite to us, where immense flocks of swans resorted every morning." His account of the expedition was included in *The Life of John James Audubon, the Naturalist*, Lucy Bakewell Audubon's 1894 biography of her late husband, some of whose wildlife art is displayed at Audubon park.

After Audubon and the Shawnee hunters reached the lake, they divided up. "As the first party fired, the game rose and flew within easy distance of the party on the opposite side," Audubon wrote. "There were plenty of ducks and geese, but no one condescended to give them a shot."

Their canoes piled high with "large, fat, and heavy swans," the Shawnees and their guest paddled away. "I have heard of sportsmen in England who walked a whole day, and after firing a pound of powder returned in great glee, bringing one partridge; and I could not help wondering what they would think of the spoil we were bearing from Swan Lake," Audubon wrote.

Almost two centuries later, Swan Lake is a safe haven for ducks and geese winging their way along the Mississippi Flyway. Long before it became a state wildlife management area, the lake may also have provided refuge to birds of a different feather.

According to a local story, Jesse James and his Missouri outlaw gang hid at the lake on one of their post–Civil War forays into Kentucky. Supposedly, Jesse marked the spot by nailing a brass martingale ornament to a tree.

Allegedly, a mysterious stranger appeared at the lake many years later. The man claimed to be related to Jesse and said he was looking for something that belonged to his notorious kinsman. Reputedly, the man hired a skiff, rowed to the far shore of Swan Lake and returned with the ornament, weatherbeaten, bearing the initials "JJ" and pierced by an old nail hole.

The Purchase Prairie

The territory was said to be "almost entirely devoid of timber, the face of the country being covered with a tall grass in which but few shrubs of any kind were to be seen, except along the streams."

Really Hidden History

Those words from J.H. Battle, W.H. Perrin and G.C. Kniffen's 1885 book, *Kentucky: A History of the State*, might summon visions of Kansas, Nebraska or other sections of the Great Plains. Yet they describe the early Jackson Purchase.

Much of the Purchase, the last part of the state settled by whites, was a prairie. "Pioneers called such grasslands in the Cumberland and Ohio Valleys 'Barrens' because there were not many trees," said Ted Franklin Belue, a Murray State University historian and author. "But 'Barrens' is a misnomer. The soil was very fertile."

The lush grasslands were home to a bounty of buffalo, elk and deer, which Native Americans hunted for food and hides. "The Indians maintained the Barrens by annual springtime burnings of the land," Belue said. "They did it for centuries."

Besides attracting game, there were many other advantages to annual firings of the grasslands, according to Belue's book *The Long Hunt: Death of the Buffalo East of the Mississippi*. "Periodically burning off broad swatches of land killed weeds and less desirable floral species, as well as lice, fleas, chiggers, ticks, and rodents…Ashes provided nutrients. Bursts of new shoots and tufts of grass created graze and browse that attracted game, especially white-tailed deer," he wrote.

Barrens blanketed other large sections of frontier Kentucky, notably in the Pennyrile region. Barren County is named for the Pennyrile grassland.

Belue said that whites discovered that while water was sometimes scarce in the Barrens, the prairies were far from infertile. The French botanist André Michaux rode his horse through prairie country in Green, Barren, Mercer, Marion and Allen Counties in 1802 and "was agreeably surprised to meet with a beautiful meadow, the abundant grass of which was from two to three feet high."

Ten years later, another traveler rode on horseback through grassland near Hopkinsville, describing it as "one vast deep-green meadow adorned with countless numbers of bright flowers springing up in all directions." He also said it would be "difficult to imagine anything more beautiful." Wild strawberries were so thick that they stained the traveler's horse's hooves red, Belue wrote.

While trees were rare in the Barrens, the tallest timber usually survived the flames, Belue said. "Where the big trees were, fires cleared out everything underneath them and created what must have looked like giant parks."

Trees were rare in the middle of the Purchase. It was said that along the Murray-Mayfield road there was insufficient timber to make even a switch.

Today, trees are common in the Purchase. But they were so remarkable in pioneer days that communities were named for them: Pilot Oak, Lone Oak,

Hickory, Brown's Grove, Lynn Grove and others. "Pilot Oak was literally a pilot oak, a landmark, on an old stagecoach road," said Graves County historian Lon Carter Barton.

While the prairie is gone, some prairie grass still sprouts here and there in the Purchase. According to an 1821 map, the biggest Barrens in the Purchase covered almost all of Graves County and parts of adjoining Marshall, Calloway and Carlisle Counties. There was a smaller grassland astride the Ballard-McCracken County line.

Belue said that by torching the prairies, the Indians practiced a form of wildlife and ecological management. "They burned off the Barrens for the same reason my dad burned off our lawn when I was a kid. It makes the grass grow better."

"Honest Abe" Beats the Rap

His nickname was "Honest Abe."

But in 1827, Abraham Lincoln ran afoul of the law near Lewisport in Hancock County. He was charged with operating a ferryboat on the Ohio River without a license but beat the rap.

Lincoln was only eighteen and too poor to hire a lawyer. Acting as his own council, he got himself acquitted by Squire Samuel Pate, a local magistrate whose log house doubled as his court.

"The squire was so impressed that he invited Lincoln to study law under him," said Marshall Myers, an English professor and author at Eastern Kentucky University. "Lincoln later said that Squire Pate was the one who got him seriously interested in becoming a lawyer."

Pate's old two-story home still stands near Lewisport. Lincoln was tried in a downstairs room, said Myers, who recounted the sixteenth president's brush with the law in his book *Great Civil War Stories in Kentucky*.

The teen had been working on a little ferryboat at Troy, Indiana, shuttling passengers to and fro across Anderson River, a tiny tributary of the Ohio. In his spare time, Lincoln built a rowboat, which earned him his first dollar. Two men asked Lincoln to row them from the Hoosier shore to a steamboat in the river. "I supposed that each of them would give me two or three bits," he said. Instead, "each of them took from his pocket a silver half-dollar, and threw it on the floor of my boat."

Lincoln could hardly believe he "had earned a dollar in less than a day… The world seemed wider and fairer before me."

Watching from the Kentucky side, ferrymen John T. and Lin Dill were hopping mad over what they saw as the loss of two customers. Brothers, the

Dills decided to teach Lincoln a painful lesson. "They planned to lure him over and beat him up," Myers said.

While John T. hid in the bushes, Lin yelled to Lincoln that he needed a ferry ride to Indiana. Unwittingly, Lincoln paddled over.

Both Dills jumped him; fists flew. "But at a strapping six-four, Lincoln proved too tough to handle," Myers said.

Battered and bloodied, the brothers turned Lincoln over to Squire Pate, demanding that the teen be punished for running an unlicensed ferry. "The charge was pretty serious," Myers said. "Lincoln could have been fined. Besides, a conviction wouldn't have looked good on the resume of a would-be president."

The Dills were Pate's pals. They were sure the squire would throw the book at young Lincoln. But the squire let Lincoln tell his side of the story.

Lincoln began by asking the magistrate for a legal definition of a ferry. Pate replied that it was a boat that carried passengers and freight from one side of a river to the other.

"Lincoln then pointed out that he hadn't carried passengers across the Ohio, only out to a boat in the middle of the river," Myers said. "Thus, he could not be guilty of operating a ferry illegally."

Pate agreed. "He complimented Lincoln on his legal reasoning and dismissed the charge," Myers said. "The Dills skulked away."

Pate kept Lincoln after court, encouraging him to become a lawyer. "The squire invited Lincoln back to witness other trials and study his law books," Myers said. Pate believed Lincoln possessed "a brilliant mind with strong determination, but with very little opportunity."

Ten years after Lincoln was hauled into court in his native state, he was admitted to the bar in Illinois. Also in 1837, he got elected to the Illinois legislature, the first rung on a political ladder that led to the White House.

"One of the Earliest Railroads in Ky"

When Jacob Van Meter, James Rumsey Skiles and their associates opened the Bowlinggreen Portage Rail Way Company, they advertised free rides for everybody in town.

"People in Bowling Green like to claim the Portage as the first railroad in Kentucky," said Nancy Disher Baird, a retired archivist, author and historian at Western Kentucky University. "Some say that claim is off the track."

Collins's *History of Kentucky* says the Portage line was more than a mile long and built about 1832, making it Kentucky's first railroad. But *The Kentucky Encyclopedia*

Portage railway marker at the Warren County courthouse, Bowling Green.

claims that the General Assembly chartered the steam engine–powered Lexington & Ohio Railroad in 1830, establishing it as the state's premier line.

"I'm generally skeptical about 'firsts,'" Baird said. "Who knows when the first train actually rolled down the tracks on these early railroads?"

A state historical marker at the courthouse in Bowling Green, the Warren County seat, hedges, confirming the Portage line was built in 1832 but calling

Really Hidden History

it "one of the earliest railroads in Ky." The courthouse site was a terminus of the mule-powered railway, over which passengers and freight bumped and swayed between the tiny Bowling Green depot and a warehouse and elevator on the banks of the Barren River.

"The river was navigable for small steamboats in those days," Baird said.

No trace of the Portage Rail Way survives. But old records at the Kentucky Library on Western's nearby campus say the Portage was more of a tramway and not much like the busy CSX Railroad, which bisects Bowling Green, commonly spelled "Bowlinggreen" in the town's early days.

"The ties were first of nondescript timber, but later red cedar was substituted," John B. Rodes wrote of the Portage line long after it was gone, probably in the 1930s. "The rails were light and somewhat flat, and the cars were horse- or mule-drawn."

The cars were small and reportedly made of iron. "A poor old mule pulled a heavily loaded iron cart up an incline from the river to the center of town?" Baird wondered. "What a pull."

Sometimes, the beasts of burden hauled more than paying passengers and freight. Boys sometimes stole rides. Baird says a letter from an early Bowling Green woman tells about a youngster who lost his grip and fell off. The car ran over his foot, and he lost a toe.

In 1836, the legislature granted a charter to Vanmeter, Skiles, James G. Potts and their business associates to build tracks "together with such wharves or landings, warehouses and depots, as may be necessary to receive and shelter goods at either end of the road."

"But the railroad could have been in operation long before it was chartered," Baird said. "There's no way to know for sure."

At any rate, Skiles evidently was one of the town's most popular citizens, according to a 1902 Bowling Green women's college literary magazine. "A Mr. Gaines...was such an admirer of Mr. Skiles and the new railroad, that he named one of his daughters, Octavia Atchison Vanmeter Skiles Portage Railroad Depot Gaines!" the magazine said.

Baird said Skiles had worked hard to improve navigation on the Barren, a narrow, swift stream that flows into the Green River northeast of Bowling Green. He rounded up volunteers to saw away overhanging trees and clear snags. "Young men came in from the country with their rations and axes, and after working sixty days—often up to their necks in water—Barren river was cleared to a sufficient extent to admit the passage of a small boat to the Double Springs landing (near where the Portage railroad ended)," the magazine reported.

When the Louisville & Nashville (L&N)—the predecessor of the CSX—pushed through Bowling Green in 1859, the company bought the Portage Rail Way and eventually abandoned the old line. But an L&N spur runs along a short stretch of the old Portage right of way, Baird said.

The Portage Rail Way again made news locally in 1921, when workers paving a Bowling Green street unearthed some of the old cedar crossties. "The ties were well preserved and were split up and divided among local souvenir hunters," the *Park City Daily News* reported.

The newspaper also claimed another first for the Portage. The *News* said the line was reputedly "the first tramway in the United States to be equipped with iron cars."

"Bleeding Yourself Dry Is Indeed a Unique Way of Maintaining One's Honor"

Few Kentucky duels were bloodier or more bizarre. Weapons weren't the usual pistols at dawn. "A scalpel was used," Odell Walker said.

"The challenged party named the terms," according to Collins's *History of Kentucky*. "They should meet at Dr. N's office, and be bled. Dr. N. opened a vein for each, and they bled until, becoming extremely weak and looking as pale as a corpse, they pronounced themselves satisfied."

Apparently, nothing else is known of the May 10, 1852 bloodletting in Eddyville. "Dueling was illegal, which might be why the duelists and the doctor weren't named," Walker said.

He suspects the physician was Dr. William C. Noel. "The 1850 U.S. census lists him as living in Eddyville, which was then in Caldwell County," Walker said. "Lyon County was created in 1854."

Duelists often hired physicians to render first aid. Bleeding was a common nineteenth-century medical practice for curing patients, not for abetting affairs of honor.

Evidently, the Eddyville combatants observed the code duello, a set of rules imported from Europe for gentlemanly one-on-one fighting. "The challenged has the right to choose his own weapon," Rule 16 said.

Bryant suggests that the anonymous Eddyville duelists were doctors themselves or were otherwise connected with the medical profession. "Most of the time the weapons of choice had a meaning to one or both of the duelists," he said.

Bryant agreed that the Eddyville duel was "definitely stranger than most" but added, "There have been as many strange duels as strange duelists." He said injured honor was avenged with axes, blunderbusses, bows and arrows, crossbows, knives, clubs, pitchforks, rocks and whips.

"But bleeding yourself dry is indeed a unique way of maintaining one's honor," he added.

"The Drinking Gourd" Pointed to Paducah

A famous folk song that supposedly helped slaves escape had a Paducah connection.

"Follow the Drinking Gourd" told slaves to track the North Star to "where the little river meets the great big river." That meant the junction of the Tennessee and Ohio Rivers at Paducah.

Here, according to the tune, "the old man is a-waiting for to carry you to freedom." He was said to be Peg Leg Joe, the song's composer.

Little is known about Joe, a one-legged sailor whose last name is evidently unknown. It has been claimed that the old salt was only a legend.

But "Follow the Drinking Gourd" was well known in the Underground Railroad, a secret organization of whites and free blacks who helped slaves get away to the North and to Canada.

The song is reportedly filled with coded messages that mapped a freedom trail along the Tombigbee, Tennessee and Ohio Rivers. Joe named his tune for the Big Dipper, which slaves called the "Drinking Gourd." The familiar constellation points to the North Star.

"Slaves viewed the North Star as a symbol of freedom and a guide for escaping," said Duane Bolin, a Murray State University historian and author. Runaway slaves usually traveled at night and hid in the day.

Folklorist H.B. Parks researched and wrote about "Follow the Drinking Gourd" in the 1920s. He heard African Americans, including a Louisville man, singing the song. B.A. Botkin included Parks's story in *A Treasury of Southern Folklore*, published in 1949.

Peg Leg Joe apparently lost his right leg at sea. He lived near Mobile, Alabama, according to Parks. Joe risked his freedom to free others. Had he been caught, he likely would have been imprisoned.

Parks said Joe drifted from plantation to plantation working as a carpenter or painter. His real purpose was to teach slaves "Follow the Drinking Gourd."

Joe showed potential escapees a print "of his natural left foot and the round spot made by the peg-leg," Parks wrote. Afterward, he would slip away north, marking an escape route on dead trees and "other conspicuous objects" with "a print made with charcoal or mud of the outline of a human left foot and a round spot in place of the right foot."

"Follow the Drinking Gourd" warned slaves to stick by the Tombigbee to the river's headwaters "between two hills." Beyond lay the Tennessee. (The two rivers are now connected via the Tennessee-Tombigbee Waterway.)

Presumably, Joe's signs pointed escapees over the hills to the Tennessee and along the northward-flowing river to Paducah, where he allegedly hid them in a boat and rowed them across. North of "the great big river" were the free states, where more "conductors" on the Underground Railroad aided escaping slaves.

Parks insisted that Joe was genuine. He said his great-uncle was in the Underground Railroad and told him Joe was cited in the records of the American Anti-Slavery Society. Joe evidently blazed his last trail in 1859, according to Parks.

Follow the Drinking Gourd is also a children's book, which includes the words to the old song.

"We Remember People Who Die in Wars, but We Forget the Animals"

He was apparently the only casualty in the Battle of Paducah to be buried where he fell. His name is not known. The grave is unmarked and all but forgotten. It might even be under a busy downtown street.

"Everybody knows that Roy Rogers's horse is stuffed somewhere or other," says Penny Baucum Fields, curator at Paducah's Market House Museum. "But almost nobody knows where Colonel Albert P. Thompson's horse is buried."

A Yankee cannonball killed the horse and its Rebel rider. Thompson died instantly. His mount "ran half a block to Sixth street and fell, and was later buried where its gallant rider lost his life in sight of his home," wrote Fred G. Neuman in his 1922 book, *Paducahans in History*.

For several years, a Kentucky historical society marker at 514 Park Avenue stood over the grisly spot where Thompson perished. Reputedly, the cannonball took his head off in the 1864 battle.

The marker was moved around the corner to 628 North Sixth Street when Park Avenue was curved to become part of the city's Downtown Loop. "The grave could even be beneath the street," Fields said.

The olive green metal tablet tells about Thompson but not his steed. "The horse should be remembered because he sacrificed his life, too," Fields said.

Really Hidden History

Paducah marker near where Colonel Thompson died and his horse was fatally wounded.

Thompson, a Paducah lawyer, had donned Confederate gray in 1861. He survived Shiloh and other bloody battles before returning home on March 25, 1864, with General Nathan Bedford Forrest's two-thousand-man cavalry army.

The Rebels, many of them local men, hit town in search of supplies. Forrest raided the Ohio riverfront with about five hundred men. Thompson, thirty-five, took the rest and stormed Fort Anderson, a cannon-bristling, dirt-walled bastion the Yankees built to protect Paducah. A pair of gunboats, the *Paw Paw* and *Peosta*, backed up the fort from the nearby river.

Union cannon and rifle fire stopped the Confederate assault against the fort, which was only a few blocks from Thompson's home. The colonel was planning his next move when, according to Neuman, Thompson "was literally torn to pieces" by a thirty-two-pound cannonball that "struck him while [he was] mounted on his favorite steed."

Thompson was buried in Paducah but reinterred near Murray, where he was born. In part, his epitaph reads, "Fell at Paducah in view of home, in the midst of his neighbors, he laid down his life."

Neuman said the colonel was popular with his men. Thompson possessed "a compelling charm of manner and an earnestness and sincerity that won instant admiration and endeared him to his comrades in arms," according to the author.

A few other books have been written about the history of Paducah. But only Neuman's book says that Thompson's horse was buried near where Thompson fell. Fields says the animal deserves more notice.

"We remember people who die in wars, but we forget the animals that also lose their lives," Fields said. "They are the innocent victims. They don't have bones to pick with anybody on either side in a battle."

Have You Heard the One about the Old De Soto They Found at Wickliffe?

"The handle of the sword is pure gold, at the top of which is a large diamond clustered around with rubies. On the handle is the name, 'Hernando de Soto.'"

Or so the old *St. Louis Globe-Democrat* reported in 1891. According to the newspaper, more than De Soto's weapon had been unearthed at the site of old Fort Jefferson near Wickliffe. Nearby were the bones of the famous Spanish explorer, plus his body armor.

The newspaper story is all but forgotten. That's probably just as well since it was bogus.

Historians are pretty sure that De Soto's final resting place is under the Mississippi River and a long way from the old fort site.

Because De Soto's exact burial spot is unknown, De Soto grave legends abound. For the record: historians say De Soto's soldiers weighted his body and tossed it in the river many miles south of Wickliffe. The Spaniards didn't want their leader's corpse falling into the hands of Native Americans who did not take kindly to Europeans killing their friends and families and stealing their land.

The *Globe-Democrat* story was well traveled. It appeared in many newspapers across America. Even some Canadian papers published it.

Supposedly, the bones, rusty body armor and bejeweled sword were accidentally discovered by men excavating an ancient Indian mound near the site of Fort Jefferson, which General George Rogers Clark built in 1780 "to protect claim of the infant United States' western boundary on the Mississippi River," according to a state historical marker close by on U.S. Highway 51.

Hernando De Soto. *Courtesy of the Library of Congress.*

"As this part of the Mississippi Valley abounds in Indian mounds, the workman supposed he was digging into" a mound, the *Globe-Democrat* said. The worker thought he had found the body of a Revolutionary War or Civil War soldier. The Yankees built a second Fort Jefferson on the spot.

"As the workman proceeded with his labor he threw up a steel breastplate and helmet," the St. Louis paper explained. "These were almost eaten up with rust and through the holes in the helmet could be seen the gray bones of a fast-decaying skull."

The sword reportedly was so rusty that it couldn't be unsheathed. "The handle and the scabbard were made of a strange composition that rust had but little effect upon, and they seemed but slightly injured by time," the paper said.

The *Globe-Democrat* also reported that inscribed on the jewel-studded sword handle was De Soto's name and coat-of-arms depicting a spring flowing from a hillside. Allegedly, the sword handle bore the Latin motto:

Hidden History of Western Kentucky

The site of Fort Jefferson, where De Soto's sword supposedly was unearthed.

"The Spring of Youth."

The newspaper also opined that "these few bones and implements of war are no doubt all that remains of the great De Soto, who believ[ed] that somewhere in the New World was a spring which bestowed upon any one who bathed in its crystal waters eternal youth." Even so, the Fountain of Youth legend is more commonly connected with another Spaniard, Ponce De Leon, and another future American state, Florida.

De Soto and his six-hundred-man army landed in Spanish Florida in 1539 and traipsed across the South to the Mississippi River. De Soto crossed the waterway in 1541, crossed back in 1542 and died of fever, probably in what is Louisiana today.

Apparently, the *Globe-Democrat* story is the only record of the purported discovery of De Soto's long-lost grave. What became of what was said to be his body, the armor and the sword is evidently unknown.

Really Hidden History

BUCKSKIN BILL'S WILD WEST SHOW

Paducah was never cowboy country. Even so, the McCracken County seat was home to America's biggest Wild West show in the early 1900s, according to John Robertson. "That's because the Buffalo Bill and Pawnee Bill Wild West shows were touring Europe," he explained.

Dubbed *Buckskin Bill's Wild West Show*, Fletcher and his brother Ed Terrell's traveling troupe is all but forgotten. "It seemed to be jinxed," Robertson said.

Terrell employees were accused of murder, attempted murder, arson and kidnapping. A star of the show died in a freak accident.

A spectator was shot to death in one performance. A doctor dodged bullets in another. A sideshow artiste tried to kill herself.

In the end, two real Wild West outlaws-gone-straight bought into the show. When they lost money, they closed the show at gunpoint.

Terrell's travails started in 1900. Four of his "cowboys," including a Terrell teenager, shot it out with a group of men defending rowdies who tried to cut through the tent and sneak into a show at Marion.

Terrell's troupers slew one man. But they pleaded self-defense and were released.

Later that year, twenty-five employees sued Terrell when he wouldn't pay them. Angry litigants supposedly burned Ed Terrell's Ballard County barn and some Paducah buildings, apparently including a theater connected to the brothers.

The firebugs also allegedly hatched "a deep, dark, and shrewdly concocted plot…to assassinate Mr. Fletcher Terrell," the *Paducah Sun* claimed. Terrell was not harmed, but one of the alleged assailants, while boozing in a bar, bragged that "they would probably have put his 'lights out,'" the *Sun* said.

Undaunted, Fletcher hit the road again in 1901. "Bad luck continued to plague the show," Robertson said.

A rehearsal before a Vincennes, Indiana performance claimed the life of Theressa Russell, "Queen of the Cowboys." "When her pony threw her, she caught her foot in the stirrup, and she was dragged to her death at age eighteen," Robertson said.

In 1902, a trio of Chicago investors bought the show. "It opened in Paducah as the largest of its kind in the nation," Robertson said. "An added attraction was the new 'steam piano' played by Colonel Bud Horn of Nashville."

Trouble trailed the show's new owners. A man in the audience was gunned down during a performance in Sturgis.

At Springfield, Tennessee, a young snake handler, jilted by her lover, shocked a crowd of one hundred spectators when she tried to commit suicide by downing a bottle of laudanum. "Only prompt effort saved the life of the girl," Robertson said.

Traveling on a train through Indiana, some men from the show coaxed a waving fifteen-year-old girl aboard their car. "Citizens of Vanceburg reported her as being kidnapped and threatened to lynch those involved," Robertson said.

In 1903, two of the Chicagoans sold out to ex-desperadoes Cole Younger and Frank James, Jesse's brother. The troupe became *The Great Cole Younger and Frank James Historical Wild West Show*, but only briefly.

Younger and James folded the show, according to Robertson. "The partner agreed only after Frank pulled a revolver to prove he was serious," the historian said.

To "Improve the Well-Being of Mankind"

A monument to Julius Rosenwald's work for "the well-being of mankind" is preserved on the Logan County High School campus near Russellville.

It is a tribute in white clapboards and big, bright windows, not stone or bronze. "So far as we know, we have the only Rosenwald School preserved as a school anywhere," said Carolyn Garrett. She is a former teacher and librarian, Logan County Retired Teachers Association member and was one of the first unofficial museum guides.

An early twentieth-century president and part owner of Sears, Roebuck and Company, Rosenwald started a foundation that provided millions of dollars to help start more than fifty-three hundred small, rural, mostly one-room "Rosenwald Schools" for African American children. They were built in fifteen southern and Border States, including Kentucky.

Kentucky was home to 152 Rosenwald Schools, as well as some homes for African American teachers, according to Dr. Alicestyne Turley, professor of pan-African studies at the University of Louisville. "We are unsure as to how many actually remain," she said, adding that Logan County had nine schools, more than any other county. Turley added that Rosenwald funds also were used to build at least three cottages for teachers in places where housing was denied them.

Logan County's Schochoh Rosenwald School was reopened as a museum in 1992. The county Retired Teachers Association spearheaded the project,

Julius Rosenwald. *Courtesy of the Library of Congress.*

raising $20,000 in donations and winning a $10,000 grant from the Kentucky Bicentennial Commission. Old records show that the county school board spent $1,652 in Rosenthal funds on the school in 1929, when segregation was the law in Kentucky.

"Public education was separate and unequal," said John Hardin, a Western Kentucky University historian and author. Hardin added that, per pupil, the state spent considerably less on African American schools than on white schools. "Kentucky was very reluctant, very parsimonious, when it came to educating blacks."

The story was the same elsewhere in the Jim Crow South, Hardin added. So in 1917, the Julius Rosenthal Fund was created to help fill the money gap. Rosenthal said he wanted to improve "the well-being of mankind"; the fund provided about $63 million for the betterment of rural education, race relations and African American health education, according to the *Encyclopedia of Southern Culture*.

Garrett said that several Rosenwald Schools were built in Logan County. The Schochoh School in south Logan County was open until the 1950s, after which local schools were desegregated. The Schochoh School became a community center and then was abandoned.

Turning the old schoolhouse into a museum on the modern high school campus required a move of about twenty miles. "They put it on a flatbed truck and brought it here," Garrett said.

It was not an easy trip to the high school, which is east of Russellville on U.S. Highway 68/Kentucky Highway 80. "They moved it in stages, once at midnight around the square in Russellville to avoid traffic," said Garrett, who helped supervise the school's relocation. "The mover was really nice,"

Logan County's preserved Rosenwald School.

she said with a smile. "It was like I was hanging a picture. I'd say, 'Here. No, there. No, back where you had it.'"

Ultimately, the old school was eased onto brick foundation pillars, after which work crews and volunteers—including retired teachers—went to work on the spruce up. Fresh paint and a new corrugated roof went on; new window glass went in.

Open by appointment, the little museum traces the history of local education from Logan County's earliest days. Furnishings range from a rough pioneer-style split-log school bench to sturdy wood and wrought-iron desks that hearken to turn-of-the-century times.

Garrett said the museum is more than relics and exhibits. "School groups come out for field trips. The GED graduates have had their graduation ceremony there. School classes have had reunions, and there have been family reunions."

WHEEL'S BIGGEST WHEEL

It's been a long time since there was even one store in Wheel, the Graves County hamlet whose favorite son grew up to be vice president.

Really Hidden History

Above: "The Veep" and the site of his homeplace. *Courtesy of Fred Biggs.*

Below: Barkley's homesite and marker.

The late Jackie Biggs said people attracted to the boyhood home of Vice President Alben Barkley sometimes had a hard time believing he ever lived so far off the beaten path.

"I don't know how many of them I've heard say, 'If this place is where Mr. Barkley was born, it's sure a long way from where he ended up,'" Biggs said.

Better known as "Mama" Biggs, Jackie lived in a little white house on the site of Barkley's birthplace, a two-story log cabin owned by his grandfather. A small gray granite monument in the front yard marks the spot. Alben Barkley Road runs past.

Barkley and a crowd at the Graves County Courthouse in Mayfield.

"People used to come out all the time and see the marker," said Fred Biggs, her grandson. "But they don't much anymore."

Nicknamed "the Veep," Barkley was vice president under Harry Truman. He had been Senate majority leader and a congressman from Paducah, to which he moved and became a lawyer.

A dirt road led to Wheel when Barkley came into the world on November 24, 1877. Wheel had a couple of stores, including a post office.

Wheel isn't easy to find unless you know the territory. It is between Fancy Farm and Lowes in northwest Graves County.

Kentucky has a bounty of little communities like Wheel. But Wheel's name and famous offspring make it unique.

In his folksy 1954 autobiography *That Reminds Me*, Barkley explained that Wheel "was named after an influential farmer of the same name, who founded a semi-secret agricultural organization known as the Wheelers." The Wheeler movement, a reflection of late nineteenth-century rural populism, established local chapters called "Agricultural Wheels" in farming communities.

Really Hidden History

Barkley's father was a staunch Wheeler, according to his son, who was elected to the Senate in 1926 and stayed until 1948, when he was elected vice president.

Jackie Biggs said Barkley visited Wheel many times. Her house contained lumber from the old Barkley cabin, which was razed many years ago.

"There was a big tree in the front yard which Mr. Barkley would say he played under as a boy," said Biggs, who treasured a scrapbook that bulges with newspaper clippings and photos of Barkley. One photo in the album, which Fred Biggs has, shows the Veep standing next to what is apparently the tree.

Biggs said people have come from across the country and even around the world to see where Barkley was born. "They'd say, 'We want to walk where he walked,'" she said.

Jackie Biggs voted for Barkley several times but confessed she never cared as much for politics as her late husband, a staunch Democrat.

"He had his politics, and I had my scrapbook," she said. "Mr. Barkley looked through it once and said it was even better than one he hired a man to keep for him."

About the Author

Berry Craig is a professor of history at West Kentucky Community and Technical College in Paducah and author of *True Tales of Old-Time Kentucky Politics: Bombast, Bourbon and Burgoo*, *Hidden History of Kentucky in the Civil War* and *Hidden History of Kentucky Soldiers*, all from The History Press. He received the annual Richard H. Collins Award from the Kentucky Historical Society in 2001.

Visit us at
www.historypress.net